SHOWDOWN
WITH
IRAN

SHOWDOWN
WITH
IRAN

Nuclear Iran and the Future of Israel, the Middle

East, and the United States in Bible Prophecy

MARK HITCHCOCK

EMANATE
BOOKS

Published in Nashville, Tennessee, by Emanate Books, an imprint of Thomas Nelson. Emanate Books and Thomas Nelson are registered trademarks of HarperCollins Christian Publishing, Inc.

Thomas Nelson titles may be purchased in bulk for educational, business, fund-raising, or sales promotional use. For information, please e-mail SpecialMarkets@ThomasNelson.com.

Unless otherwise noted, Scripture quotations are taken from New American Standard Bible®. Copyright © 1960, 1962, 1963, 1968, 1971, 1972, 1973, 1975, 1977, 1995 by The Lockman Foundation. Used by permission. (www.Lockman.org)

Scripture quotations marked ESV are from the ESV® Bible (The Holy Bible, English Standard Version®). Copyright © 2001 by Crossway, a publishing ministry of Good News Publishers. Used by permission. All rights reserved.

Scripture quotations marked KJV are from the King James Version. Public domain.

Scripture quotations marked NIV are from the Holy Bible, New International Version®, NIV®. Copyright © 1973, 1978, 1984, 2011 by Biblica, Inc.® Used by permission of Zondervan. All rights reserved worldwide. www.Zondervan.com. The "NIV" and "New International Version" are trademarks registered in the United States Patent and Trademark Office by Biblica, Inc.®

Scripture quotations marked NLT are from the Holy Bible, New Living Translation. © 1996, 2004, 2007, 2013, 2015 by Tyndale House Foundation. Used by permission of Tyndale House Publishers, Inc., Carol Stream, Illinois 60188. All rights reserved.

Any Internet addresses, phone numbers, or company or product information printed in this book are offered as a resource and are not intended in any way to be or to imply an endorsement by Thomas Nelson, nor does Thomas Nelson vouch for the existence, content, or services of these sites, phone numbers, companies, or products beyond the life of this book.

ISBN 978-0-7852-3448-7 (eBook)
ISBN 978-0-7852-3447-0 (TP)

Library of Congress Control Number: 2020931106

Printed in the United States of America
HB 06.06.2022

To my daughter-in-law Ellen
You're a wonderful blessing from God to Samuel, but also to me
and our entire family beyond anything we could ask or think.
I thank God every day for making you part of our
family and bringing your radiant joy into our lives.

CONTENTS

BEYOND THE HEADLIGHTS

Not long ago I found myself driving down the interstate between Oklahoma City and Dallas in the worst rainstorm I've ever experienced. Darkness and driving rain descended like a heavy blanket. Traffic slowed to a crawl as drivers strained to see the road or anything in front of them. Everything was covered in a sheet of rain. All I could see was the hood of my car. Automobiles and trucks, trying to avoid slamming into each other, were pulling over and stopping beneath underpasses because they couldn't see even a few feet beyond the headlights. Fortunately, I was among those able to find sanctuary to wait out the storm.

Have you ever been there? Traveling down the road, straining and longing to see beyond the headlights, to see what's ahead. If only you could know what's coming next—could know or predict what lies just in front of you or just around the next bend in the road. Everywhere we look today our world appears more and more like a dark storm with a drenching downpour.

The sky is black and threatening. In the dark, uncertain days of the storm in which we live, we all long to see beyond the headlights, to know, to have some sense of where things are headed to calm our troubled hearts.

Is there a reliable source to show us what lies ahead? To shine through the darkness?

A SURE WORD

The biblical prophets of old claimed to know the future, including the final series of apocalyptic events that will bring this age to its stunning climax. By consulting their predictions, you and I can know the future of people and nations, because world events—including current events—are part of a larger story scripted ahead of time.

We don't have to follow their predictions blindly. We can put their prophecies to the test because hundreds of them have already been literally fulfilled with 100 percent accuracy. The Bible, which was 28 percent prophecy at the time it was written, is the only book in existence with a long, extensive track record of accurately predicting the future. The best estimates are that the Bible contains about one thousand prophecies. Up to now, five hundred of those have been literally, precisely fulfilled. With that performance history we can be sure that the Bible's unfulfilled prophecies will come to pass just as surely and literally as those that have already been fulfilled.

For this reason, through the centuries, people from all walks of life and backgrounds have turned again and again to the Bible's ancient end-time prophecies to discover God's plan for human history. By studying the ancient writings, we can know the pattern of events foretold by the prophets long ago and written in Scripture.

As we turn to the pages of Scripture today, we discover that as unsettling and alarming as current events are, they shouldn't surprise us in light of end-time prophecy. The escalating crisis we see today in Iran and the Middle East is a buildup to the events of the end times predicted in Scripture. Events in the Middle East are unfolding just as we should expect if we consult the biblical end-time template.

We can't be sure how long the buildup will last. It could be nearing its end or just beginning. But we do know that events in our world today, especially in the Middle East, strikingly foreshadow the prophecies laid out in the pages of Scripture. Current events are casting end-time shadows. The number of prophetic signposts is multiplying. The harmony of today's headlines and current events with Scripture suggests that end-time biblical prophecies could be fulfilled at any time.

Through God's Word we can see beyond the headlights. But what can we see?

FROM HEADLIGHTS TO THE SPOTLIGHT

Scripture shines a prophetic spotlight squarely on the Middle East, especially on the nation of Israel, but also on those who oppose Israel at the end of days. The scriptural spotlight reveals a cast of characters and places imbedded in a storyline that is part of the script that moves the biblical story to its predicted climax.

Prominent in this story is Iran, which is arguably the world's most dangerous, provocative nation. The Islamic Republic of Iran is the world's number one sponsor of terror. Its tentacles reach throughout the Middle East.

Authors Charles Dyer and Mark Tobey have observed:

Since the founding of the Islamic Republic, Iran has displayed a consistent commitment to two major goals. The first is to support the expansion of militant Islam, especially Shiite Islam. Iran's unflagging support for the Houthis in Yemen, Hezbollah in Lebanon, the Shiite militias in Iran, and Bashar al-Assad in Syria all share this in common.

Iran's second goal is the destruction of Israel, which they refer to as the "Zionist entity" and the "Little Satan". . . . The world might not take its threats seriously, but Iran has made no secret of its ambitions. Iran's leaders want to re-create the Persian Empire of old, but with an Islamic twist. They desire an arc of Shiite control stretching from Iran to the Mediterranean. They hope to become the dominant Muslim power in the Middle East . . . But to reach that goal they need to find a way to eliminate Israel.

And that is where Iran's desires may intersect Bible prophecy.[1]

Succinctly stated, that's what this book is about: *the intersection of current events in Iran and the Middle East with Bible prophecy.* The following chapters will demonstrate that the converging and aligning of current events corresponds with the prophetic preview presented in Scripture.

As we observe and evaluate current events and world headlines, there are three key factors to keep in mind. First, the world is ever changing. Change is the new constant. There will be many twists and turns in the days ahead. We must be careful not to speculate about every interesting headline and its possible role in the end times.

Second, we must always evaluate current events in light of the Bible, and not the other way around. The Bible is our fixed point. To accurately discern if and how any current events fit into the prophetic picture, we need to understand Bible prophecy.

Third, events we see today are not the final fulfillment of Bible prophecy. The curtain has not been raised on God's drama of the ages. God is still setting the stage behind the curtain, providentially moving the props and players into place. When everything is finally in place and the time is right, the curtain will go up.

The raising of the curtain will take place, suddenly and without warning, at an event called the *rapture*, which is described in 1 Thessalonians 4:16–17 and is the next event on God's prophetic calendar. At the rapture, Jesus Christ, the Son of God, will come for His church, those who have believed in Him for salvation. In the time it takes to blink, He will meet His people in the air and whisk them away to heaven. The rapture is an imminent, unannounced event. No prophecy remains to be fulfilled before we could see the rapture. It could happen at any time—possible any day, impossible no day.

The curtain can go up at any moment.

THE EDGE OF TOMORROW

When it happens, the rapture will shock the world, because unexpectedly, millions of people will simply be missing. Spouses and children, rich and poor, soldiers and pastors, beggars and businesspeople—gone without a trace. As you can imagine, in the aftermath, people will search for some semblance of stability and security. The world will be gripped with fear. Confusion will reign. Then a strongman, known in Scripture as the Antichrist, will arise amid the chaos from a Western confederacy, with answers and solutions. He'll be the man with a plan. He will ascend on a platform of peace and will forge a seven-year peace pact for Israel and her neighbors, one that will bring a palpable harmony to the Middle East. The Antichrist will be hailed by the world. He may even win the Nobel Peace Prize. Under his treaty, for the first time in her modern history, Israel will let down her guard and depend on the West for security. People everywhere will enjoy peace and safety . . . yet it will be but the calm before the storm.

From that point on, a series of catastrophic events will engulf the world. A Russian-Iranian alliance including other Islamic nations will attempt to deliver a final, crushing blow to Israel, only to be supernaturally destroyed. This will pave the way for the balance of power to swing decisively in favor of the Western leader—the Antichrist. He will break the seven-year treaty with Israel at its midpoint and quickly begin consolidating power. During the final three and a half years of what is known as the Tribulation period, he will rule the world politically, militarily, and religiously. He will even go as far as to deify himself and demand worship. In the meantime, a series of devastating geological and ecological disasters will pummel the planet. The end of days will climax at the final great Battle of Armageddon, when Jesus returns to defeat the Antichrist and his forces and establish His righteous kingdom on earth for one thousand years.

As astounding as the prophecies are, world events are moving toward their fulfillment. Nations are moving into place. World events are setting the stage. The escalating crisis in the Middle East fueled by Iran is an integral part of the buildup.

SEARCHING FOR ANSWERS

Everywhere we turn ancient prophecies are pregnant, ready to deliver and give birth to the end of the age, raising a chorus of compelling questions.

- Are current events in Iran and the Middle East part of a larger drama scripted long ago?
- Does the Bible predict the rise of Iran in the end times?
- What about Syria, Turkey, and Russia in the end of days?
- Where's the current crisis headed?
- Will Israel survive?
- What role, if any, will America play in the end of days?
- How should we live in light of current events?

As Christians, are we discerning enough to know what's coming? Will we be ready? Will you be ready? Bible prophecy was not given to scare us but to prepare us. It was not given to make us anxious but to make us alert and aware.

Two days before He died, Jesus told His closest followers, "Be on guard! Be alert! You do not know when that time will come." Then, comparing Himself to a master on a journey, He added, "Therefore keep watch because you do not know when the owner of the house will come back—whether in the evening, or at midnight, or when the rooster crows, or at dawn. If he comes suddenly, do not let him find you sleeping. What I say to you, I say to everyone: 'Watch!'" (Mark 13:33, 35–37 NIV).

Jesus wants us all to live looking.

The following pages are intended to increase your watchfulness and awareness of what lies ahead and to prepare you for the coming of Jesus. It is my hope that they will help you live faithfully in the meantime as you look for the end time—as you endeavor to see beyond the headlights.

So, grab your Bible, and let's get started.

CHAPTER 1

COUNTDOWN TO CRISIS

Peace with Iran is the mother of all peace.
War with Iran is the mother of all wars.
—Iranian president Hassan Rouhani,
New York Times, August 6, 2019

[The US] may have to get in wars. . . . If Iran does
something, they'll be hit like they've never been hit
before. I mean, we have things that we're looking at.
—President Donald J. Trump

The showdown between the United States and Iran became a shooting war that spiraled out of control on June 20, 2019. . . . *Almost.*

In response to Iran shooting down an American drone, the United States was ten minutes away from striking three Iranian bases with air- and sea-launched missiles. The United States and Iran were on the brink of war—on the verge of US bombs raining down on Iranian soil. As zero hour was imminent, in the nick of time, President Trump aborted the attack.[1] Yet it appears that war was only suspended to a later date. It could break out at any moment. Iran and the United States remain locked in a serious showdown.

The threat level was so serious that "the Pentagon presented the White House with plans for deploying up to 120,000 troops to the Middle East to respond to Iranian attacks on US forces or the acceleration of Iran's nuclear weapons program."[2] According to *Foreign Policy* magazine, "since May [2019], the Pentagon has dispatched 14,000 additional US troops, an aircraft carrier, and tens of thousands of pounds of military equipment to the Middle East to respond to what it says are alarming new threats from Iran."[3] An ominous ABC News headline tells the story: "The Shootdown Showdown Between US and Iran."[4]

Adding to the tense standoff, Iranian limpet mines exploded on two oil tankers in June 2019, leaving them crippled and burning in the Gulf of Oman. In response, President Trump sent 1,000 additional troops to the Middle East. Iran is the reason for the reinforcements.

Later in the troubled summer of 2019, an American warship in the Persian Gulf, the USS *Boxer*, shot down an Iranian drone. As the standoff intensified and the tension mounted, on November 2, 2019, President Trump issued a warning against Iran in a tweet based on the HBO show *Game of Thrones*. The tweet contained a picture of the president with a caption in the show's recognizable font, "Sanctions are Coming November 5." Within hours, Iran responded with its own *Game of Thrones*–inspired tweet against an eerie background that read, "I will stand against you." On his Instagram page an Iranian commander posted, "Come! We are waiting. I can stop you. . . . You start this war, but we will finish it."[5]

The Middle East game of thrones is a modern Game of Drones.

On the nuclear front, which carries the greatest potential for disaster, the United States unilaterally backed out of the 2015 Iran nuclear deal, the JCPOA (Joint Comprehensive Plan of Action) and re-imposed crippling sanctions on Iran in a campaign of "maximum pressure." Iran's reaction was swift. Tehran boldly escalated its nuclear pursuits, quadrupling its uranium production. Iranian centrifuges are spinning at a record pace. The nuclear breakout time span is shrinking every day. As of the writing of this book, Iran could have a fully functional nuclear weapon in seven to eleven months. More and more, this looks like a pivotal year. Tectonic shifts are transpiring in the Middle East.

Iran has threatened to treat any nation as an aggressor that even cooperates with the United States.[6] Many experts maintain that Iran will keep escalating its aggression in the Persian Gulf and Middle East until the United States hits them back hard or folds.

The United States and Iran have been at war with each other for more than forty years, but the cold war threatened to become a hot war at the advent of 2020. Iran orchestrated an attack against the US embassy compound in Baghdad, Iraq. Iranian-backed Shiite militants stormed the massive 104-acre embassy, chanting "Death to America" while setting fires and destroying property. The siege came in response to US strikes in Iraq against Iranian proxies that had killed a US contractor and injured others.[7] One hundred US Marines were immediately dispatched to Baghdad to increase security.[8] An additional 750 paratroopers from the US Army's Eighty Second Airborne Division's alert brigade were deployed to Kuwait.[9]

This was the second time a US embassy came under attack by Iranian terrorists. The first time was in Tehran in 1979 during the Islamic Revolution, which precipitated the Iran hostage crisis. Both President Trump and Secretary of State Mike Pompeo warned that Iran would be held accountable, and that accountability came swiftly. An American drone attack ordered by the president killed Iranian major general Qasem Soleimani, commander of Iran's elite Islamic Revolutionary Guard Corps's Quds Force. Soleimani was responsible for planning and executing extra-territorial military activity for Iran and enjoyed near-celebrity status in Iran. He was arguably the most powerful military leader in the Middle East and—with the exception of the supreme leader, Ayatollah Ali Khamenei—was the most important person in Iran.

Iran immediately threatened revenge. President Trump warned that any loss of US lives would bring swift and devastating reprisal. Headlines across the country announced that President Trump had declared war on Iran.[10] The world held its collective breath. The words "World War III" were trending. In an effort to save face, but not further arouse the ire of the United States, Iran fired a few missiles at an Iraqi base that housed Americans, but there were no casualties. However, fifty US soldiers required medical treatment for traumatic brain injury. Again, war was averted at the last minute. The tension was temporarily released.

But what will happen next time?

Unquestionably, there's a growing sense of urgency. The clock is ticking. The crisis continues to brew. Major conflict looms in the Middle East. American sentiment is not optimistic. The American public expects the United States and Iran to go to war in the near future. According to a national opinion poll, 41 percent of adults in the United States consider Iran to be an "imminent threat," up 17 points from a similar poll in May 2019. The poll also found "that 71 percent of Americans believe that the US will be at war with Iran within the next few years, up 20 points from May's poll," and that 27 percent of Americans are in favor of a "preemptive attack" or first strike on Iran's military.[11]

PROPHETIC FLASH POINTS

The United States and Iran, however, are far from alone in the surging showdown. The Middle East neighborhood has become very crowded in the last few years, increasing the chances and raising the stakes for a major regional conflict as nations and terror groups stake out their turf and jockey for position.

Saudi Arabia and Iran, close neighbors across the Persian Gulf, are mortal enemies and are at each other's throats. They narrowly avoided war in September 2019 when twenty Iranian drones and cruise missiles obliterated the Saudi Aramco oil processing facility, the world's largest, in Abqaiq, Saudi Arabia. The attack cut Saudi Arabia's oil production in half, shaking global oil markets. Some Israeli strategists call this surprise attack the Middle East's "Pearl Harbor."[12] Saudi Arabia seriously contemplated a military response but decided against it. For now.

In response to the attack, President Trump said, "Saudi Arabia oil supply was attacked. There is reason to believe that we know the culprit, [and] are locked and loaded. . . . I'm not looking for war, and if there is, it'll be obliteration like you've never seen before."[13] The United States deployed troops to Saudi Arabia for the first time since 2003, putting them in harm's way of Iranian missiles. One careless move on either side could spark a response that sets the region aflame.

Iran is the puppet master for a growing list of loyal proxies, contracting out much of its dirty work to these surrogates who are entrenched all over the Middle East. Iran activates these insurgents when needed. Iran provides essential training, funds, and arms to its growing list of militias. Hezbollah, Iran's most prominent proxy, is the tip of the spear for Iran. Hezbollah and Israel have traded blows and been on the verge of war for years, but one more reckless move on either side could ignite the tinder box. Iran's other main proxy, Islamic Jihad in Gaza, fires rockets into Israel daily and stands ready to escalate its aggression at any time.

Underlying all of Iran's aggression is a dark, apocalyptic religious ideology that's deeply held by the mullahcracy that runs the nation. Their messianic belief in the return of the Mahdi, who they believe will come in time of warfare and bloodshed, fuels their reckless desire to spark a confrontation with the United States and Israel, activating the apocalypse.

Syria's brutal civil war, raging since 2011, has pitted government loyalists against rebels. Iran has taken advantage of the conflict in Syria to move into the chaos. As the Syrian civil war rages on, Iran has leveraged instability there and in the rest of the Middle East to expand its footprint in the region.[14] Iran has moved in and is constructing a huge military base in Syria, entrenching its presence and spreading its arc of influence to Israel's northern doorstep.[15] This presence affirms Iran's long-term strategy remains unchanged—the destruction of the Jewish state.

Russian influence in the Middle East is deepening and expanding at the same time US influence is waning. Moscow seems to have its fingerprints in every Middle East nation to one degree or another. Most importantly, Russia has joined Iran in Syria, raising the anxiety level and potential danger for Israel.

Even Turkey, in alliance with Iran and Russia, has moved into Syria to attack the Kurds in an offensive called Operation Peace Spring. Russian and Turkish troops, working in concert, control a broad corridor in northeastern Syria. Turkey is also involved in Libya and Iraq, expanding its footprint.

As you can see, potential, prophetic flashpoints abound. The drumbeat of war reverberates through the Middle East. One wrong move could set off a firestorm. All signs point to an imminent conflict. A buildup is brewing. At the center of the showdown stands Iran. Tehran's fingerprints can be found in the Strait of Hormuz, Yemen, Iraq, Lebanon, Gaza, and Syria. Everyone knows war is coming to the Middle East. The showdown could become a shootout at any moment.

ISRAEL IN THE CROSSHAIRS

Meanwhile, Israel sits at the epicenter of the region watching alarming events unfold around them as Iran steadily besieges and encircles Israel in what's called the "ring of fire."[16]

Israel and Iran are squared off in a death struggle that threatens to spiral out of control. The noose is tightening around Israel as Iran is developing sophisticated missile technology and racing toward the nuclear finish line. An Israeli think tank warned that there's a "growing risk of a large scale war along Israel's northern border in the next year."[17]

In Israel, the normal attitude of preparedness is quickly shifting to alarm. Israel knows it must act against Iran. Israel can't let a nation that daily calls for its destruction get its hands on a nuclear missile. The winds of war are swirling. Storm clouds are gathering. Rumors of wars abound. Israel and Iran are on a collision course. War is coming. It's not a matter of *if* but *when*. Referring to Iran and Israel, Seth Cropsey, senior fellow at the Hudson Institute in Washington, DC, says it bluntly, "War will come—if not now, then soon."[18]

A steady stream of ominous world headlines underscores the snowballing showdown with Iran.

"The US-Iran Showdown," *Washington Post*, June 21, 2019

"The Israel-Iran War Is Here," *Wall Street Journal*, August 27, 2019

"Waist Deep and Sinking in the Middle East: We're Now at War with Iran," *The Hill*, January 4, 2020

"The Coming Middle East Conflagration," *Atlantic*, November 4, 2019

"Trump and Iran May Be on a Collision Course, and It Could Get Scarier," *New York Times*, June 19, 2019

"The Israel-Iran Shadow War Escalates and Breaks into the Open," *New York Times*, August 29, 2019

"US and Iran on the Brink of War," ABC News, January 5, 2020

"US-Iran Crisis: Pompeo Sends Chilling Warning to Iran—'Time Is Running Out,'" *Daily Express*, August 13, 2019

"Iran Entrenches Its 'Axis of Resistance' Across the Middle East," *New Yorker*, September 19, 2019

As *New York Times* columnist Thomas L. Friedman says, "Everyone is recalculating: The Iranians are emboldened, the Arabs are frightened, and Israel and Iran are one miscalculation away from a war of precision missiles that neither can afford.[19] World leaders talk about restraint, diplomacy, and avoiding confrontation, but that can shift suddenly to a rush to war. A regional conflict can erupt at any moment. The countdown has begun. The countdown to conflict for sure . . . but could it also be a countdown to something even greater? A countdown to the prophesied apocalypse? Could what's unfolding point toward the fulfillment of ancient prophecies found in the Bible?

WHAT'S NEXT?

What will happen next time the United States and Iran find themselves at the brink of war? Will war be postponed or pursued? Will the United States stand down again when the next Iranian provocation occurs, or will the United States unleash fury? In a US presidential election year, will Iran sense American reluctance to go to war?

Will an emboldened Iran interrupt the world's oil supply by shutting down the narrow chokepoint known as the Strait of Hormuz through which 15 percent of the world's oil supply moves every day, touching off a US military response? Will Iran use Hezbollah or Hamas (which occupies land situated on Israel's southwest border) to provoke a confrontation with Israel?

Feeling more and more threatened, Israel has launched more than one thousand attacks on Iranian positions in Syria, Lebanon, and Iraq in the last two years to contain Iran's buildup. Iran won't take this forever. It is deeply embedded all over the Middle East, biding its time to get even. Iran is itching to strike back against Israel.

At any moment, Israel may feel compelled to launch a preemptive, "preventive" strike against Iran to prevent it from gaining sophisticated missile capability and crossing the nuclear finish line. If Israel senses that something ominous is at hand, a preemptive strike such as the one in June 1967 against Egypt, initiating the Six-Day War, could be repeated against Iran. Israel faces an existential threat from Iran. She might act despite knowing that a preemptive strike against Iran raises the specter of a protracted and punishing regional war.[20]

At any point, the Russian bear could lose patience and assemble its allies to overrun the Middle East, putting Israel in the crosshairs. Iran could leverage its military presence in Syria and its numerous well-armed militias to launch an assault against Israel.

The biblical prophets tell us that war is coming to the Middle East.

We're witnessing the buildup.

But what's the next move?

CHAPTER 2

ATOMIC IRAN AND THE APOCALYPSE

*The Islamic Republic of Iran's nuclear program
no longer faces any operational restrictions.*

—Iran's official news service

Appearing on NBC's *Meet the Press* in 2006, when asked what would happen if Iran gets the nuclear bomb, Senator John McCain responded, "I think we could have Armageddon."[1] Undoubtedly, he expressed the fear of many people if Iran were to go nuclear. Few events would change the world as dramatically as Iran getting its hands on a nuclear weapon. Israel would immediately face an existential threat. Iran's supreme leader, Ayatollah Khamenei, regularly spews out statements like this: "The belief that Israel must be eliminated is a condition of our adherence to Islam . . . Each and every one of our officials should reiterate our responsibility of the need to destroy this cancerous tumor of Israel."[2] This leaves little doubt of what Iran would do if it obtained the bomb, and recent events are propelling Iran much closer to the nuclear threshold than ever before. Eric Brewer and Ariane Tabatabai say it bluntly: "Iran is back in the nuclear game."[3]

Iran's nuclear program took a giant leap forward after the US drone strike killed Iranian Major General Qasem Soleimani in Baghdad. In the wake of his death, Iranian President Hassan Rouhani's administration said, "The country will not observe limitations on its enrichment, the amount of stockpiled enriched uranium as well as research and development in its nuclear activities." Iran has pulled back from the nuclear deal commitments and is now enriching with no restrictions. All bets are now off with Iran's nuclear program. The most recent estimates are that Iran's nuclear-breakout time line is now reduced to only seven to eleven months.

The now infamous Iran nuclear deal that was endorsed by UN Security Council Resolution 2231 and adopted on July 20, 2015, is dead. President Donald Trump ditched the deal in May 2019 when the United States unilaterally withdrew from the nuclear accord. In response, Iran stepped up its production of nuclear material and began testing faster centrifuges to accelerate the fuel-producing process.[4] Since the death of Soleimani, Iran has thrown off all shackles.

In addition to the existential threat this poses for Israel, if Iran obtains nukes, most experts believe it will throw the door wide open for an all-out nuclear arms race in the Middle East—a chain reaction—with Turkey and Saudi Arabia following close behind. Iran is the fuse on an explosive nuclear powder keg. On January 23, the *Bulletin of the Atomic Scientists* moved the hand on the iconic "Doomsday Clock" to one hundred seconds before midnight, the symbolic hour of the Apocalypse. This is the first time the countdown has been expressed in seconds rather than hours or minutes. According to the *Bulletin*, doomsday is closer than it's ever been since the clock was created in 1947.

Another dangerous angle is that for some time North Korea has been a key supplier of missile technology to Iran. This raises the fear that Iran could procure a ready-made nuclear weapon from North Korea.

US Secretary of State Mike Pompeo sounds the alarm: "Iran's expansion of proliferation-sensitive activities raises concerns that Iran is positioning itself to have the option of a rapid nuclear breakout."[5] The time required for a nuclear breakout varies depending on the expert, but all agree that the interval is shrinking quickly, especially in light of recent developments. Some months ago, a *World* magazine headline caught my eye: "Countdown: Will Iran Have a Fully Functional Nuclear Missile in 2020?" (July 20, 2019).

No one knows the answer to this question, but even the suggestion should set off alarm bells in Israel and the United States. As Israeli Major General Yaakov Amidror said, "There is a strong connection between a nuclear Iran and the ring of fire around Israel. With a nuclear umbrella, Iran would be free to build a ring of fire around Israel" at which point, it would be too late for Jerusalem to stop either the nuclear program or Iran's destabilizing behavior in the region.[6] That means time is running out for Israel to deliver a deterring blow. How far will the United States and Israel allow things to progress before initiating a first strike to set back Iran's nuclear quest?

Iran's Nuclear Timeline[7]

1987	Iran acquired nuclear centrifuge technology from Dr. Abdul Qadeer Khan, a renegade Pakistani engineer.
January 1995	Russia signed an $800 million nuclear plant deal with Iran to complete the nuclear plant at Bushehr.
November 2004	Iran agreed to suspend uranium enrichment.
January 9, 2006	Rebuffed by European diplomatic efforts, Iran resumed uranium production at its plant in Natanz, claiming that its only intention was to make reactor fuel to generate electricity.
March 29, 2006	The UN Security Council unanimously approved a statement demanding Iran suspend uranium enrichment.

April 9, 2006	Iran officially announced it had begun enriching uranium.
2009–2012	Rounds of sanctions and talks are conducted.
2012	Talk of an Israeli strike against Iran escalates amid renewed negotiations and strengthened sanctions.
2015	The heralded Joint Comprehensive Plan of Action (JCPOA), also known as the Iran nuclear deal, is signed by Iran and the P5+1 (United States, United K, France, China, Russia, and Germany).
2019	The United States backs out of the JCPOA and reinstates crippling economic sanctions on Iran. In response, Iran escalates its nuclear production.
2020	Iran pulls back its commitments to the nuclear deal in the wake of the US drone strike against Major General Qasem Soleimani, further reducing the time for a nuclear breakout to less than a year.

DECADES IN THE MAKING

Iran's love affair with the bomb goes back decades, at least to the 1980s. The United States and European nations have continuously pursued discussions, negotiations, and concessions with Tehran but with few lasting results. Iran clandestinely works on its nuclear program and employs a strategy of "talk and build." Using this tactic, Iran delays and strings along negotiations as it continues to advance toward the nuclear finish line.

TOXIC TALK

As Iran works feverishly to procure a nuclear weapon, its leaders talk daily about wiping Israel off the map. That's a potentially lethal combination. Here's just a small sample of what Iran's leaders, and leaders of Hezbollah, in Lebanon, have said about Israel. If you're Israel, these are not people you can allow to get the bomb.

> Ayatollah Ali Khamenei: "It is the mission of the Islamic Republic of Iran to erase Israel from the map of the region."
>
> Hassan Nasrallah, leader of Hezbollah: "If they [Jews] all gather in Israel, it will save us the trouble of going after them worldwide."
>
> Nasrallah: "Israel is our enemy. This is an aggressive, illegal, and illegitimate entity, which has no future in our

land. Its destiny is manifested in our motto: 'Death to Israel.'"

Mohammad Hassan Rahimian, Khamenei's representative to the Moustazafan Foundation: "We have manufactured missiles that allow us, when necessary, to replace Israel in its entirety with a big holocaust."

Mohammad Reza Naqdi, commander of the Basij paramilitary force: "We recommend them [the Zionists] to pack their furniture and return to their countries. And if they insist on staying, they should know that a time will arrive when they will not even have time to pack their suitcases."

Khamenei: "The Zionist regime is a cancerous tumor and it will be removed."

Hossein Salami, the deputy head of the Revolutionary Guard: "We will chase you [Israelis] house to house and will take revenge for every drop of blood of our martyrs in Palestine, and this is the beginning point of Islamic nations awakening for your defeat."[8]

Hossein Sheikholeslam, a foreign affairs adviser to parliamentary speaker Ali Larijani: "Our positions against the usurper Zionist regime have not changed at all; Israel should be annihilated and this is our ultimate slogan."[9]

These are just a few of the thousands of poisonous statements that continue to spew forth from Iran and its proxies. You can almost feel the venom dripping from the page as they beat the drum for a second holocaust. There's no reason for any peace talks or diplomacy with enemies who call you a "cancerous tumor" and lick their chops at the thought of seeing you liquidated, all while seeking a nuclear weapon that can bring their hatred to fruition.

COUNTDOWN 2020

The year 2020 has a special ring to it. It instantly brings to mind the thought of perfect vision. Many are tapping in to 2020 for all kinds of marketing strategies. Some prophecy teachers can't resist the temptation to tie 2020 to the fulfillment of biblical prophecies.

The Bible never sets dates for any end-time events. Neither should we. In fact, Scripture strictly forbids any kind of date-setting for the end times or the coming of Jesus. Even so, there are some key markers in 2020 that could propel the Middle East showdown to all-out war. Several factors point to 2020 as a potentially critical year in the showdown with Iran.

First, the New Year—2020—began with the United States taking out the second most important man in Iran—Qasem Soleimani. The blowback from this will continue into 2020 and beyond as Iran and its proxies have revenge on their minds.

Second, there's an international arms embargo on Iran that will be lifted in October 2020. From that point, Iran will be able to arm to the teeth. Russia and China are lining up to sell arms of all kinds to Iran. There's no doubt Iran will seek new advanced fighter jets and other military hardware, including tanks and Russia's S-400 air defense system. Israel's window to deliver a strong military setback to Iran is closing. US Secretary of State Mike Pompeo said, "Time is running out on the international agreements restraining the Iranian regime. . . . Soon after, the Iranian regime will also be free to sell weapons to anyone, including terrorist proxies, and countries like Russia and China will be able to sell the Iranian regime tanks, missiles, and air defense equipment."[10] After October 2020 the situation in Iran will change dramatically. Israel knows this and is weighing its options.

Third, Iran is working toward advanced missile and drone technology at the same time it's pursuing the bomb. In addition to giving Iran a viable threat against the United States and Israel, possessing nuclear weapons will boost Iran's global image as a major player—recognition Iran eagerly seeks. Nuclear missiles will boost Iran's claim to hegemony in the region and will encourage its leaders to pursue even more aggressive and adventurous policies with respect to Israel. Such policies will be advanced by a coalition of terrorist groups, equipped with thousands of state-of-the-art missiles under a nuclear umbrella.

Both the United States and Israel have said repeatedly that they won't allow Iran to get a nuclear weapon or even get close to the threshold. If Iran's breakout time for a nuclear weapon shrinks much further, a preemptive, preventive strike by Israel could be imminent, provoking a punishing retaliatory strike from Iran that could quickly spiral out of control, engulfing the entire region.

Fourth, Iran may sense US weakness to retaliate against any aggression during a presidential election year. The *Wall Street*

Journal notes: "This danger is likely to increase in an election year in several theaters where adversaries may test Mr. Trump's resolve. Iran is feeling the pressure of US sanctions and may believe that attacking Americans will coax the president to ease the pressure."[11]

President Trump has expressed continued reluctance to get enmeshed in more wars in the Middle East. He wants to withdraw the US from "forever wars." However, at the same time, he ordered the killing of General Soleimani and has sent more US troops to the region. Iran could take advantage of these mixed signals and the increasing desire for US isolationism by carrying out more acts of aggression and provocation to spur US isolationist impulses. In addition, the division and distraction in Washington over impeachment and its fallout could give Iran an opening. Michael Oren, former Israeli ambassador to the United States observed, "Back in 1973, Egypt and Syria saw a president preoccupied with an impeachment procedure and concluded that Israel was vulnerable. In the subsequent war, Israel prevailed—but at an excruciating price. The next war could prove even costlier."[12] Iran's political calculation could lead to something significant in 2020.

Fifth, as noted previously, Iran is suffering under crippling economic sanctions from the United States. Iran's currency, the rial, has lost 60 percent of its values against the dollar. Oil sales have plummeted 80 percent. Iran's economy is in a death spiral. Its mullahs could feel cornered and lash out in desperation, believing they have little to lose to gain some kind of concessions.

Sixth, due to deteriorating economic conditions, Iran is

experiencing the worst unrest it's seen since the days of the Islamic revolution forty years ago. Spiking gasoline prices sparked riots, but overall worsening economic conditions have triggered protests by citizens and violent responses from the regime. Protests in Lebanon and Iraq have also erupted. If the situation in Iran doesn't settle down, the mullah regime could impetuously strike Israel or US assets in the Middle East to shift the focus off problems at home and unite the nation against a common enemy. As Iran reels under the weight of several crises, the Ayatollah told the nation they are living through "days of God."[13]

No one knows for sure if 2020 is the key year for a wider conflict with Iran, but the tension can't be sustained at this level much longer. Something has to give. The risk of an all-out conflict with Iran is casting its shadow over 2020 . . . and beyond.[14]

HOT-WIRING THE APOCALYPSE

The danger of Iran obtaining a nuclear weapon is exacerbated by the apocalyptic religious ideology that holds its leaders in its grip. The Iranian ayatollah and sinister mullahs hold to an alarming, eerie "Apocalypse Now" viewpoint. They're waiting for the return of their Mahdi or messiah, known as the "Twelfth Iman."

They believe they can accelerate the end of days and their final victory by creating chaos and bloodshed. Part of hastening the apocalypse is getting rid of the "Great Satan" (America) and the "Little Satan" (Israel). This adds a much deeper dimension to Iran's vitriol toward the United States and Israel, and Iran's nuclear pursuits. The clash is not just about power and geography, it's about Iran's realizing its messianic destiny.

Writing in the *Jerusalem Post*, Lela Gilbert unmasks the apocalyptic madness that undergirds Iran's pursuit of the bomb and overall aggressive posture.

Why does Iran continue to saber-rattle and threaten to massacre Israelis? Why do Iranian religious and military leaders constantly vow to impose terrible violence on their enemies? And why is the ever-escalating aggression carried on by various Iranian proxies across the Middle East? These days, international commentators assume that threats of violence and warnings of war are Iran's boastful way of defying US economic sanctions, which presently have a strangle-hold on their leaders and institutions. Meanwhile, disturbances in the Persian Gulf have underscored the Islamic Republic's rage at America's withdrawal from the JCPOA. But there is, perhaps, another reason as well—an apocalyptic belief that is widely held by Iran's supreme leader and his followers.

Gilbert further states:

The Hidden—or Twelfth—Imam plays a dominant role in one specific form of Shi'ite Islamic theology, called "Twelverism," which happens to be the primary belief system of Iran's leadership. There is a messianic belief that at the end of days, the Hidden Imam will appear in the midst of a violent apocalyptic scenario played out on a battleground stained with infidels' blood. . . .

[Iranian scholar Saeed Ghasseminejad wrote,] "While many experts tell us Iran is a rational, pragmatic regime like any other in the world, all the facts shout that it is not. A large number of Iranian officials and decision makers have deeply rooted apocalyptic beliefs. Underestimating this radical ideology even as the Iranian regime is on its way to building a nuclear bomb can lead to dangerously wrong conclusions. The suggestion taking hold of late that a nuclear armed Iran is not the end of the world may unfortunately be dead wrong."[15]

Israeli poet and writer Salman Masalha puts it poignantly: "The Islamic revolution, which brought the ayatollahs to power in Iran, awakened messianic demons from their sleep."[16] These awakened demons are on full display in Iran today. Those who understand the nexus between Iran's nuclear pursuits and its messianic demons have an additional incentive to keep Iran from getting weapons of mass destruction.

THE SYRIAN CONNECTION

Iran's growing presence in Syria also plays into its apocalyptic views and desire for nuclear weapons. Iran is present in Syria for many reasons—nearness to Israel's northern border, support for Bashar al-Assad (Syria's president) in the civil war that's raged there since 2011, and the desire for a Shia crescent from Iran to the Mediterranean. However, an often forgotten or overlooked reason for Iran's presence in Syria is the messianism that grips Iran's menacing mullahocracy. According to the strain of Islam practiced in Iran, Iran's messianic hopes find their fulfillment in Syria.

> Syria is important to Iran for messianic reasons because according to Shi'ite traditions, the Mahdi's reincarnation is associated with a bloody civil war that will take place in Syria and cause hundreds of thousands of deaths. It begins on a small scale then escalates. Every time it seems to be calming down in one area, it bursts out in another, until the Mahdi appears. . . .
>
> When the Shi'ite Mahdi appears, he will bear God's explicit name in Hebrew. He will also hold Moses' staff, wear Solomon's seal and carry the Israelites' Ark of the Covenant, in which the Divine Presence (*shekhina*) dwells. With the ark with the Divine Presence he will conquer cities and countries and impose law and justice in the world.[17]

Iran's growing presence in Syria is the realization of a long-awaited hope. Iran believes events are unfolding in keeping with their view of the end of days. Appendix 2 provides more detail about biblical prophecy related to Syria and its capital Damascus in the end times.

CONVERGING CONNECTIONS

Iran is taking aggressive action to bring about the realization of its future. Syria, a mullah regime, the Ayatollah, nuclear weapons, a violent end-of-days scenario, and intense hatred for Israel and the United States are all essential ingredients in this apocalyptic vision. At some point these ingredients will mingle in a toxic cocktail that will set in motion a series of events that will propel the world toward the fulfillment of ancient biblical prophecy. Events are converging right on schedule.

But before we turn to the ancient forecast of the Hebrew prophet Ezekiel, there's one more volatile ingredient to add to the mixture.

CHAPTER 3

DIRE STRAITS

If someday, the United States decides to block Iran's oil
[exports], no oil will be exported from the Persian Gulf.
—IRANIAN PRESIDENT HASSAN ROUHANI

It's not going to be closed for long . . .
They're not going to be closing [the strait].
—PRESIDENT DONALD TRUMP, ON IRAN
CLOSING THE STRAIT OF HORMUZ

According to the dictionary *dire straits* means "a state of extreme distress . . . a bad or difficult situation or state of affairs."[1] That's an apt description of the world's direst "strait": a situation in Iran's backyard—involving the Strait of Hormuz—or SOH. A dark shadow looms over the waters of the strait as massive tankers traverse its narrow channel under Iran's watchful eye. Iran regularly threatens to close the strait in retaliation against US actions. This could be called the "Iranian shutdown" as the Strait of Hormuz is frequently crawling with Iranian speedboats that stand ready to swarm hostile vessels, shutting off the spigot of oil from the Persian Gulf. The Strait of Hormuz is a perennial international hotspot. It's been the focal point of US-Iranian confrontations for more than thirty years.

What makes it such a frequent flashpoint that shows up in the news on a regular basis?

The Strait of Hormuz is the number one shipping channel in the world. The narrow strait, which connects the Persian Gulf and the Gulf of Oman, lies along the western coast of Iran. Ships traversing the strait must pass through Iranian waters. It's the only sea passage from the oil-rich Persian Gulf to the open ocean. And Iran believes it owns the strait.

The SOH is a vital gateway for global oil supply. According to the *LA Times*, "The Strait of Hormuz is the busiest, most important waterway for the world's oil industry. More than a third of the world's seaborne oil passes through the strait."[2]

The United States Energy Information Administration (EIA) estimates that 18.5 million barrels of oil pass through the Strait of Hormuz each day. It is "the world's most important chokepoint. . . . More than one-fourth of all global liquid natural gas exports and various consumer goods pass daily through the Strait."[3]

The SOH is ninety-six miles long and twenty-one miles

wide at its narrowest point; however, the shipping lanes in each direction are just two miles wide. This narrow area of operation provides Iran a major tactical advantage, making it easy to saturate with mines and swarm with speedboats.

RECENT CONFLICT IN THE STRAIT OF HORMUZ

Several recent clashes have highlighted the ongoing hostility in the SOH. In the tension-filled summer of 2019, six oil tankers came under attack. Two were damaged by explosions after leaving the strait. Four were struck while within the United Arab Emirates territorial waters. Iran diverted a British-flagged oil tanker to one of its ports—an action the UK called illegal—and shot down a US drone over the strait. The United States downed an Iranian drone that came too close to the USS *Boxer*. This dangerous "Game of Drones" inched the United States and Iran closer to a shooting war. Iran's provocative actions are stoking the fires of open conflict. The United States has promised to strike back hard if Iran takes any similar actions in the future. To back up that threat, the US has sent an additional fourteen thousand troops to the region, including an aircraft carrier.[4]

The narrow strait is the launch point for Iran's aggression and pushback for Western economic sanctions. Iran is desperately seeking leverage, a bargaining chip, for any future nuclear negotiations as well as flexing its muscles to show it can disrupt global oil flow by choking off the Persian Gulf. More provocative action by Iran is expected.

To make matters even more complicated, Russia and China have joined Iran in naval war games in the Gulf of Oman just outside the SOH. This joint exercise boosts Iran's image as a regional power.

THE TANKER WAR

Skirmishes in the Persian Gulf between the United States and Iran are nothing new.

What we see today evokes memories of the tanker war more than thirty years ago when the SOH was the scene of a tense standoff between the United States and Iran.[5] During the 1980s, 40 percent of the world's oil passed through the Strait of Hormuz, so any disruption, no matter how slight, threatened to create chaos in the global oil market.

The tanker war was waged from 1984 to 1988 during the Iran-Iraq War as Iran picked off Kuwaiti vessels transporting Iraq's oil to market. Kuwait persuaded US President Ronald Reagan to reflag and escort its vessels through the Strait of Hormuz. In the spring of 1988, an Iranian mine disabled and nearly sank the USS *Samuel B. Roberts*. In response to Iran's actions, open conflict between the United States and Iran erupted on April 18, 1988. The United States waged an intense one-day battle against Iranian forces in and around the strait. The US-Iran shooting match resulted in the disabling of several Iranian warships.

In some ways the tanker war between the United States and Iran never ended. It was just indefinitely suspended. Both sides stopped shooting, but nothing was really settled or resolved. It was simply a perilous prelude to what's happening in the Persian Gulf today and what will inevitably persist in the future.

FROM PRELUDE TO PROPHECY

The Strait of Hormuz remains at the center of escalating US-Iranian tensions. From the tanker wars in the late 1980s to the 2020s, the SOH has been and continues to be a major danger zone. One reckless move by either side could reignite the thirty-year-old confrontation, picking up where it left off, but this time the stakes are much higher than in 1988. Iran is emboldened by its military advances throughout the region and filled with more than thirty years of built-up animosity toward what it calls the "Great Satan." Iran is locked and loaded in the SOH. Iran appears to have a sense of security and daring when acting so close to home.

Never missing an opportunity to threaten Israel, Iran has exploited any potential problems in the SOH to issue a serious warning to Israel. Hossein Amir-Abdollahian, special aide to the president of the Islamic Parliament, said that if Israel ever gets involved in any conflict in the Straits of Hormuz, then "it will be engulfed in wrath of the region and its smoke will rise from Tel Aviv."[6]

Iran has proven time and again that it will seize on anything in the SOH to justify further acts of belligerence. As Iranian Foreign Minister Mohammad Javad Zarif warned recently, "We always respond. Don't play with Iran."[7] While talk like that can be viewed as simply more Persian bluster and bravado, Iran's "eye-for-an-eye" strategy of payback seems to be for real in the SOH more clearly than anywhere. By all appearances the SOH will continue to be a critical staging ground for potential conflict between the United States and Iran for the foreseeable future. At the same time, it will undoubtedly play a significant role in the ongoing tension as the Middle East buildup to the end times gains momentum.

CHAPTER 4

THE PERSIA PROPHECIES

The past is never dead. It's not even past.
—WILLIAM FAULKNER, *REQUIEM FOR A NUN*

I n his play *The Tempest*, Shakespeare's character Antonio utters the now-famous words, "What's past is prologue." In contemporary use, the phrase means that history creates the context for the present. That what has happened in the past sets the stage for the present and future.

What's true in general is especially true in biblical prophecy. Historical events often set up the future and even repeat themselves. They recapitulate and replicate established patterns. Biblical prophecies dealing with Persia are no exception. Iran's past is prologue to what we see today, and also to what's coming in the future.

The ancient Persian Empire was impressive. It conquered Babylon, under the rule of King Cyrus and ruled over a huge swath of territory for about two hundred years (539–331 BC). The empire rule over two million square miles, stretching from Egypt to India. As we're witnessing Iran's attempt to birth a new Persian Empire, it's important to briefly look back at biblical prophecies about Persia that have already been fulfilled to see what they can tell us, if anything, about what we see today and what we can expect tomorrow.

PRESENTING PERSIA

The word *Iran* never appears in the Bible in any end-time prophecies, but the name of its ancient counterpart, *Persia*, in its various forms, is found thirty-six times in the Old Testament. In recent times the name Persia was changed to Iran, which means "land of the Aryans," and then was later changed to the Islamic Republic of Iran.

Many occurrences of the word *Persia* in Scripture are simply historical references, but there are several fascinating biblical prophecies about Persia that have already come to fulfillment. The past fulfillment of prophecies about Persia is prologue to what we see today. Knowing the literal fulfillment of past prophecies establishes the trajectory for the fulfillment of future prophecies.

DANIEL: THE RISE AND FALL OF
THE PERSIAN EMPIRE

The Jewish prophet Daniel lived in the sixth century BC during the Babylonian Empire and the early years of the Persian Empire. The book of Daniel contains three main prophecies about ancient Persia that have been fulfilled in the ancient past.

Daniel 2: Silver Shoulders

Daniel 2 recounts a dream of Nebuchadnezzar, king of Babylon, given to him by God. The meaning of the dream was interpreted by Daniel the prophet. Nebuchadnezzar's dream involved a colossal statue of a man consisting of four different metals: gold (the head), silver (the shoulders and arms), bronze (the belly and thighs), and iron (the legs). The feet of the image consisted of a mixture of iron and clay. Daniel interpreted these four metals as symbolic of four successive empires that would rule over Israel—Babylon, Persia, Greece, and Rome. The feet, with ten toes, represented a final form of the Roman Empire in the end times, under the rule of ten leaders. This has often been referred to as Rome II or a reunited Roman Empire. Many believe the European Union is an embryonic phase of this final stage of the Roman Empire.

The main point, for our purposes, is that Daniel predicted the rise of the Persian Empire while Babylon was still ruling and accurately saw the future fall of Persia to Greece. This occurred two hundred years after Daniel died.

Daniel 7: A Lopsided Bear

Daniel 7 presents the same succession of empires as in Daniel 2, but in chapter 7, Daniel uses wild animals to symbolize the empires.

> I was looking in my vision by night, and behold, the four winds of heaven were stirring up the great sea. And four great beasts were coming up from the sea, different from one another. The first was like a lion and had the wings of an eagle. I kept looking until its wings were plucked, and it was lifted up from the ground and made to stand on two feet like a man; a human mind also was given to it. And behold, another beast, a second one, resembling a bear. And it was raised up on one side, and three ribs were in its mouth between its teeth; and thus they said to it, "Arise, devour much meat!" After this I kept looking, and behold, another one, like a leopard, which had on its back four wings of a bird; the beast also had four heads, and dominion was given to it. (Daniel 7:2–6)

The bear, which symbolizes the Medo-Persian Empire is pictured as lopsided because the Medians initially dominated the empire but were eventually superseded by the Persians. All this came to pass just as Daniel predicted.

Daniel 8: A Routed Ram

The final prophecy about Persia that has already been fulfilled is found in Daniel 8.

In the third year of the reign of Belshazzar the king a vision appeared to me, Daniel, subsequent to the one which appeared to me previously. I looked in the vision, and while I was looking I was in the citadel of Susa, which is in the province of Elam; and I looked in the vision and I myself was beside the Ulai Canal. Then I lifted my eyes and looked, and behold, a ram which had two horns was standing in front of the canal. Now the two horns were long, but one was longer than the other, with the longer one coming up last. I saw the ram butting westward, northward, and southward, and no other beasts could stand before him nor was there anyone to rescue from his power, but he did as he pleased and magnified himself. While I was observing, behold, a male goat was coming from the west over the surface of the whole earth without touching the ground; and the goat had a conspicuous horn between his eyes. He came up to the ram that had the two horns, which I had seen standing in front of the canal and rushed at him in his mighty wrath. I saw him come beside the ram, and he was enraged at him; and he struck the ram and shattered his two horns, and the ram had no strength to withstand him. So he hurled him to the ground and trampled on him, and there was none to rescue the ram from his power. (Daniel 8:1–7)

This prophecy employs the image of a ram for Persia and a goat for Greece. The prophecy is amazingly specific. The ram has two horns. One is longer than the other, and the longer one came up last. The imagery is similar to the lopsided bear in Daniel 7. The goat in this prophecy overpowers the ram. The prophecy was fulfilled in the Medo-Persian Empire when the Medes, who were initially more powerful in the empire, were conquered by the Persians, and then both were conquered by Greece.

Daniel accurately predicted the details of the fall of the Persian Empire to Alexander the Great two hundred years before it happened in 334–331 BC. After that crushing defeat, Persia never rose again in history to be a great power.

Daniel's Persian prophecies were fulfilled literally and historically with 100 percent accuracy. We can put them to the test like the hundreds of other biblical prophecies that have come to pass just as predicted.

ISAIAH: THE REIGN OF CYRUS THE GREAT

Daniel wasn't alone in prophesying about Persia. Almost two hundred years before Daniel prophesied, Isaiah uttered an astounding prophecy related to Persia and its greatest leader, King Cyrus. He is referred to in Isaiah 41:2–4, 25, but in Isaiah 44:28 and 45:1, he is specifically called by name more than one hundred years before he was born. Isaiah 45:2–6 goes even further, predicting Cyrus's conquests and his edicts allowing the Jewish people to return to their land.

Isaiah 44:28 specifically foretells Cyrus's restoration of the Jews to their land and their temple worship. "It is I who says of Cyrus, 'He is my shepherd! And he will perform all My desire.' And he declares of Jerusalem, 'She will be built,' and of the temple, 'Your foundation will be laid.'" This was dramatically fulfilled in 2 Chronicles 36:22–23.

> Now in the first year of Cyrus king of Persia—in order to fulfill the word of the LORD by the mouth of Jeremiah—the LORD stirred up the spirit of Cyrus king of Persia, so that he sent a proclamation throughout his kingdom, and also put it in writing, saying, "Thus says Cyrus king of Persia, the LORD, the God of heaven, has given me all the kingdoms of the earth, and He has appointed me to build Him a house in Jerusalem, which is in Judah. Whoever is among you of all His people, may the LORD his God be with him, and let him go up!"

Interestingly, based on President Donald Trump's favorable treatment of Israel and the Jewish people, some have suggested he is a modern counterpart to Cyrus. There's no doubt President Trump has been a great friend and supporter of Israel. Every defender and friend of Israel owes the president thanks for his actions on behalf of the Jewish people and their homeland. His list of achievements is impressive. He moved the US embassy from Tel Aviv to Jerusalem (recognizing Jerusalem as Israel's capital), acknowledged the Golan Heights as part of Israel, legalized Jewish West Bank settlements, and signed an executive order that included condemnation of anti-Jewish bias as a form of discrimination.

In light of President Trump's actions and their similarity to those of Cyrus, it has been noted that Cyrus is mentioned by name in Isaiah 45 and that Donald Trump is the 45th president of the United States. Some prophecy teachers have thus projected a prophetic link between these two leaders who are separated by more than twenty-five hundred years. So, what should we make of this?

The connection is certainly interesting. I have no problem seeing President Trump as similar to Cyrus in his favorable actions toward Israel. However, any prophetic linkage based on the number 45 is tenuous at best, and speculative and sensational at worst. Additionally, even if one could make this connection, what's the point? There's no further prophecy in Isaiah 45 for President Trump to fulfill. Acknowledging that both these leaders have been used by God to bless His people is enough.

PROLOGUE IS PROOF

Ancient Persia passed off the world stage after being eclipsed by the Greek Empire under Alexander the Great, just as Scripture predicted. After being absorbed by the Greeks, Persia ultimately faded and ended up on the ash heap of history as far as being a significant world player. That condition persisted for centuries, but in the last part of the twentieth century, we witnessed the newest incarnation of Imperial Iran as Iran ascended to a place of prominence in the Middle East under the rule of the ayatollah and radical Islam. Since that time, over the last forty years, Iran has become the major actor and source of disruption it is today.

The ascent is no accident. Iran's increase is a key part of the matrix of events that are setting the stage for the end times. Its modern rise is predicted in the book of Ezekiel. The end-time prophecy found in Ezekiel 38–39 cannot be fulfilled without Iran as a military force and presence in the Middle East, and these final prophecies of Iran will be fulfilled just as literally and specifically as the ones in Isaiah and Daniel that have already come to pass.

The Bible is clear that Iran will be an integral part of a cluster of nations that will strike Israel in the end times. For the first time since Ezekiel penned his prophecy more than twenty-five hundred years ago, the necessary preconditions for its fulfillment are falling into place. The correlation between current events in Iran and the Middle East with Bible prophecy is striking.

What we see today in Iran reveals a trajectory that points toward the fulfillment of Ezekiel 38, possibly very soon.

CHAPTER 5

THE ALIGNING OF NATIONS

In the 38th chapter of Ezekiel, it says that the land
of Israel will come under attack by the armies of
the ungodly nations . . . For the first time ever,
everything is in place . . . It can't be too long now.
Ezekiel says that fire and brimstone will be rained
upon the enemies of God's people. That must mean
that they will be destroyed by nuclear weapons.
—PRESIDENT RONALD REAGAN, 1971

[T]heologians . . . studying the ancient prophecies . . . have
said that never, in the time between the prophecies up
until now, has there ever been a time in which so many
of the prophecies are coming together. There have been
times in the past when people thought the end of the world
was coming, and so forth, but never anything like this.
—PRESIDENT RONALD REAGAN, 1983

45

Two days before He died on the cross, Jesus delivered one of His greatest sermons from the Mount of Olives, just east of Jerusalem, overlooking the Temple Mount. In that sermon known as the Olivet Discourse, Jesus outlined the signs that will portend His return to earth to deliver Jerusalem and judge the world.

In His discourse, Jesus uttered these sobering words, which have been repeated countless times across the centuries: "You will be hearing of wars and rumors of wars. See that you are not frightened, for those things must take place, but that is not yet the end. For nation will rise against nation, and kingdom against kingdom" (Matthew 24:6–7). According to Jesus, the end times will be marked by military conflict. They will be fraught with feuding and fighting. Peace will be removed from the earth and replaced with bloodshed (1 Thessalonians 5:1–3; Revelation 6:1–2).

Although the end times in general will be marred by wars and rumors of wars, two great conflicts will stand out from among the rest. The first is described by the Hebrew prophet Ezekiel in chapters 38–39 of the book named for him. (See appendix 1 to read these two chapters, to get the entire context of Ezekiel's prophecy.) These chapters describe a Russian-Islamic surprise attack on Israel that will threaten Israel's very existence. We'll discuss the details of this invasion in more detail in the next chapter.

The second great war of the end of days is the Battle of Har-Magedon, or Armageddon, described in the book of Revelation:

The sixth angel poured out his bowl on the great river, the Euphrates; and its water was dried up, so that the way would be prepared for the kings from the east. . . . And I saw . . . three unclean spirits . . . go out to the kings of the whole world, to gather them together for the war of the great day of God, the Almighty. ("Behold, I am coming like a thief. Blessed is the one who stays awake and keeps his clothes, so that he will not walk about naked and men will not see his shame.") And they gathered them together to the place which in Hebrew is called Har-Magedon. (16:12–16; cf. 14:19–20; 19:11–21)

Some scholars and biblical commentators maintain that Ezekiel 38 and Revelation 16 describe the same war. However, a careful reading of the two passages reveals that they depict two different conflicts separated by some span of time.

The war of Gog and Magog, in Ezekiel 38, will occur first and will involve a limited number of specifically named nations (vv. 1–6). The Battle of Armageddon will involve all the nations of the earth, will culminate in the Second Coming of Christ to earth, and will end the time of great tribulation.

While the Battle of Armageddon must be years away, I believe the war of Gog and Magog could be on the near horizon. The current showdown with Iran strikingly foreshadows this coming war. What we see happening today is the perfect buildup. The specific countries and circumstances are converging with accelerating speed to take their prophesied places just as we should expect if this war is coming.

In the popular movie *The Lord of the Rings: The Return of the King*, the wizard Gandalf gazes ahead to what's coming and says, "The board is set, the pieces are moving. . . . We come to it at last . . . the great battle of our time."[1] In a similar way, when we look at our world, we see that "the pieces are moving." The prophesied nations are aligning before our eyes. "The great battle of our time" may be fast approaching.

IRAN RISING

According to Ezekiel's prophecy Iran will be part of a colossal end-time strike force that will move into Israel. That much is certain. Persia, or modern Iran (the name was changed in 1935), is listed in Ezekiel 38:5 as one of the nations that will participate in this last-days invasion of Israel. That means the rise of Iran in the last forty years as the world's number one sponsor of terror and Israel's public enemy number one is no accident. Iran stands poised today right on Israel's northern border in Syria. Again, no accident.

For Israel one thing is sure—Iran is coming. They won't miss the opportunity to try to wipe Israel off the map once and for all. As authors Charles Dyer and Mark Tobey wrote:

> Iran's hatred for Israel is a matter of religious conviction. They have invested uncounted billions in terror organizations and ever-more-deadly weapons of destruction, much of it intended to be used against Israel. Iran also knows its limitations and

Israel's strengths, and that has kept it from pushing Israel too far. But if Iran were ever given an opportunity to be part of a massive coalition mobilizing against Israel, their leaders would jump at the chance.

Ezekiel predicted that's exactly what they will do—when the time is right.[2]

But Iran won't come alone. Far from it. According to Ezekiel 38, a coalition of nations will join Iran's ill-fated invasion of Israel.

And the word of the LORD came to me saying, "Son of man, set your face toward Gog of the land of Magog, the prince of Rosh, Meshech and Tubal, and prophesy against him and say, 'Thus says the Lord GOD, "Behold, I am against you, O Gog, prince of Rosh, Meshech and Tubal. I will turn you about and put hooks into your jaws, and I will bring you out, and all your army, horses and horsemen, all of them splendidly attired, a great company with buckler and shield, all of them wielding swords; Persia, Ethiopia and Put with them, all of them with shield and helmet; Gomer with all its troops; Beth-togarmah from the remote parts of the north with all its troops—many peoples with you. (vv. 1–6)

The coalition presented in these verses is already loosely in place and gathering momentum. Let's briefly examine the various nations that will be part of this strike force along with Iran.

THE MAN NAMED GOG

The first proper name in Ezekiel's list of enemies is "Gog," a word found eleven times in Ezekiel 38–39. The only other references to Gog are in 1 Chronicles 5:4, which has no connection with the Gog in Ezekiel 38, and in Revelation 20:8. *Gog* may mean "height" or "mountain," or alternatively it may be related to a word meaning "darkness." Whatever the precise meaning, this name points to a dark, menacing figure. Gog will be an enemy of God and Israel.

The context of Ezekiel reveals that Gog is an individual, not a nation, because he is personally addressed by God (38:14; 39:1) and is called a prince (38:2; 39:1). Gog will be the commander of the anti-Israel coalition. Additionally, he is identified as the last-days leader of *Rosh*, which I believe refers to Russia (more about that later).

Many believe Gog is another title for the final Antichrist. I believe Gog and the Antichrist are two different end-time leaders of two separate coalitions of nations. Scripture presents the Antichrist as the head of a Western confederacy of nations sometimes called the reunited or revived Roman Empire, while, according to Ezekiel 38, Gog will preside over a Russian-Islamic bloc of nations. These men will rule over competing, opposing spheres vying for influence in the end of days.

I don't believe we should try to identify any modern leader as Gog or spend time trying to figure out the identity of the Antichrist. Trying to name the Antichrist is reckless and futile until the end times begin. In the same vein, there's no way to know for sure if the current leader of Russia is Gog. However, I find bestselling author Joel Rosenberg's words on Vladimir Putin insightful.

Putin is a power-hungry, greedy, authoritarian, Czar wannabe. He is determined to expand Russian wealth, power and control over her neighbors. He has worked especially hard to build strategic alliances with Radical Islamic leaders and states in the Middle East. Over the years, people have asked me if Putin might be the Russian dictator referred to as "Gog" in the Biblical prophecies of "Gog and Magog" in Ezekiel 38–39. . . . Here's my quick answer: It's too soon to draw such a conclusion. There's much more that would have to happen to indicate that Putin was the "Gog" of Bible prophecy. But there's no question in my mind that Putin is *Gog-esque*. He is dangerous, and both Israel and the West should keep a close and wary eye on him, especially given all that Putin has done to build a strategic alliance between Russia and Iran and the other countries mentioned in the "Gog and Magog" prophecies.[3]

At this point, it's impossible to say Putin is Gog or to conclusively say he is not. Time will tell. But I agree that at a minimum we can safely say Putin is *Gog-esque*. If nothing else, Putin serves as a forceful foreshadow of what Gog will be like when he does emerge on the world scene. Putin is a ruthless, shrewd leader who is galvanizing the Middle East under his umbrella of influence. There is growing momentum in Russia among Putin's acolytes and many others to throw off term limits and for Putin to be the permanent leader of Russia—the czar. They want a return of the monarchy to Russia.[4] Even if Putin does step down at the end of his term in 2024, as he's indicated, he is proposing changes to Russia's constitution to guarantee his continued hold on power. The *New York Times* calls him "Putin the Immortal."

Moscow's footprint has increased dramatically under Putin's leadership. His actions, especially in the Middle East, have not gone unnoticed. Speaking of Putin, France's former minister of foreign and European affairs, Bernard Kouchner said, "All the mystery and everything about the Middle East I can summarize with the name of Mr. Putin, as he is the king of the Middle East."[5] "King of the Middle East"—that's quite a moniker. But it seems to fit Putin well.

In a *Wall Street Journal* article, Jonathan Spyer dubbed Putin as "the new King of Syria."[6] Russian-Syrians ties are nothing new. Syria has been Russia's strategic partner since 1956. The unprecedented turmoil in Syria created by the civil war that began in 2011 has opened the door wide for increased Russian control. Russian presence and power on Israel's northern doorstep are striking in light of Ezekiel 38, which predicts a Russian-led invasion from the north into Israel in the last days. If not Putin, then another Russian leader like him will fulfill the Gog prophecy.

So, the first thing we discover about Iran's final showdown is that Iran will be allied with Russia. That's no stretch today, as

Iran is deepening ties with Russia. Iran has carried out naval war games with both Russia and China. When Gog comes calling, Iran will jump at the chance to join the alliance to attack Israel and wipe them out once and for all.

THE GATHERING COALITION

According to Ezekiel, Gog will assemble a massive, multi-national coalition. But as we read Ezekiel's prophecy, we need to recognize that none of the places mentioned in Ezekiel 38 can be found on any modern map. The only exception is the nation of Put, which some translate as Libya, which is known by the same name today. As we should expect, Ezekiel employed ancient place names that were familiar to the people of his day. The names of these geographical locations have changed numerous times through the millennia, and some could change again. Yet, the physical, geographical area remains the same. Whatever names these nations may bear at the time of this invasion, it's these geographical territories that will be involved. And they represent quite a diverse cast of characters.

Magog

Magog is the first of several ancient places listed by Ezekiel that are first mentioned in Genesis 10:2–4 in the Table of Nations. A fierce, warlike group of nomadic tribes known as the Scythians inhabited the land of Magog.[7] Their homeland spans from what today is known as central Asia across the southern steppes of modern Russia. Modern Magog includes many satellites of the former Soviet Union: Kazakhstan, Kirghizia, Uzbekistan, Turkmenistan, and Tajikistan. Some believe Russia may be part of ancient Magog and that it could incorporate Afghanistan. With the exception of Russia, all these nations embrace Islam. Religion is the glue that will bring them together.

Rosh

Rosh is a reference to Russia. This connection is not based on the fact the two names sound alike. That's a poor argument for equating an ancient place with a modern nation. Compelling linguistic, historical evidence exists for making this connection.[8] More than two and a half millennia ago, the prophet Ezekiel predicted that in the latter times Israel would be invaded by a people "from the distant north" or the "remotest parts of the north" (Ezekiel 38:6, 15 NLT; 39:2). Drawing a line up or north from Israel on any map leads directly to Russia. The Russian bear will be Israel's great nemesis from the north in the last days.

Since World War II, the mighty Russian bear has risen to a place of world power.

When the Soviet Union was broken up in the early 1990s, many believed that the Russian bear was retreating into permanent hibernation. Of course, Russia lost territory and influence and was temporarily weakened and humiliated. But under the leadership of Vladimir Putin, the Russian bear has come roaring back and is a much more dangerous bear than ever before. Russia has more nuclear warheads today than any nation on earth. Putin wants to lead Russia back to its former days of glory. In a speech at the Kremlin, Putin referred to the collapse of the Soviet Union as "a major geopolitical disaster of the century."[9] Implicit within that statement is that the greatest achievement of the century would be the Soviet Union's restoration. Putin longs to restore the glory days of the Soviet Empire.

Russia is gaining influence in the Middle East and the Persian Gulf. The footprints of the bear are all over the Middle East, and Putin himself is embracing the Middle East in a huge bear hug. The preparatory build up for the Gog invasion seems to be developing right before our eyes. For the first time in history Russia and Iran are allies, working together to exert influence over the Middle East. Ezekiel 38 could never have been fulfilled until the last few years. Daily headlines bear a remarkable correspondence to Ezekiel's prophecy, written more than five hundred years before the birth of Christ. This is strong support for the inspiration of the Bible. Only God can predict the future with pinpoint accuracy.

Any day now, Israel may feel compelled to strike Iran to prevent Tehran from reaching a point of military and nuclear no return. When this happens, Iran will seek revenge at all cost. Payback will be palpable. Such an attack by Israel could function as the lighting of the fuse that precipitates the gathering of the Ezekiel 38 alliance.

Ezekiel 38 pictures Russia as reluctant to lead the invasion of Israel in the end times. The prophet refers to the "hooks" in the "jaws" that God will use to pull Russia into this foray (v. 4). Pressure from Iran to punish Israel for an attack could be the force that's needed to draw Russia in. Russia has a vital stake in Iran. Its deepening connection to Iran, as well as other Middle East nations, could eventually force its hand, pulling it into leading the invasion of Israel.

Meshech and Tubal

Meshech and Tubal normally appear together in Scripture. They are mentioned two other times in Ezekiel (27:13; 32:26). Meshech and Tubal are the ancient *Moschoi* and *Tibarenoi* in Greek writings. They are the *Tabal* and *Musku* in Assyrian inscriptions. These ancient nations are located in what today is Turkey.

Ethiopia (Cush)

The Hebrew word *Cush* in Ezekiel 38:5 is frequently translated "Ethiopia" in modern English versions. In ancient times Cush was known as *Kusu* by the Assyrians and Babylonians, *Kos* or *Kas* by the Egyptians, and *Nubia* by the Greeks. Cush was consistently located directly south of ancient Egypt in what today is Sudan.

Russia's activity in Sudan is deeper than ever before. Sudan also maintains a strong partnership with Turkey. The Islamic nation is now free of any influence from the Christian south and is at liberty to act on its own. Sudan is a zealous Islamic stronghold that supported Iraq in the Gulf War and sheltered Osama bin Laden for five years in the 1990s. It stands ready to take its place in the coming Gog alliance against Israel just as Ezekiel predicted.

Libya (Put)

The Hebrew word *Put* or *Phut* is found in Ezekiel 38:5. The Septuagint, which was the Greek translation of the Old Testament, translates the word as *Libues*. For this reason, several modern translations, including the King James Version, the New King James Version, and the New Living Translation, substitute the word *Libya* in this verse. Ancient sources locate Put in North Africa to the west of Egypt. The nation immediately west of Egypt is Libya, but Put could include nations even farther west, such as Algeria and Tunisia.

Modern Libya was ruled by Colonel Muammar al-Qaddafi from 1969 until the outbreak of the revolution in 2011 during the Arab Spring when he was violently killed. Since that time Libya has descended into chaos. Presently, two rival factions are dueling for power in a bloody civil war. Turkey is supporting one side in the conflict and sending troops to Libya.[10] Russia is helping the same faction. Moscow is assuming a growing role in Libya's war. These deepening connections with Turkey and Russia will prove instrumental in drawing Libya into the coalition to invade Israel when the time comes.

Gomer

While some prophecy teachers erroneously equate Gomer with modern-day Germany, Gomer represents the ancient Cimmerians, or *Kimmerioi*. According to ancient sources Gomer is associated with the Akkadian *Gi-mir-ra-a* and the Armenian *Gamir*. From the eighth century BC, the Cimmerians occupied territory in Anatolia, which makes up the majority of modern Turkey. The Jewish historian Josephus stated that the Gomerites were equated with the Galatians, who inhabited central Turkey.[11]

Beth-Togarmah

Beth-Togarmah means the "house of Togarmah." The ancient Assyrians referred to Togarmah as *Til-garamu*, while the Hittites used the word *Tegarma*. Either way, the territory of Togarmah is located in modern Turkey, which is north of Israel.

As you can see, four of the names in Ezekiel 38:1–6 refer to Turkey—Meshech, Tubal, Gomer, and Beth-Togaramah. Turkey is an ally of Iran and an avowed enemy of Israel. Under Recep Tayyip Erdoğan, who assumed the Turkish presidency in 2003, Turkey has taken a strong turn toward dictatorship and an adamantly anti-Israel posture. His opposition toward Israel is straightforward: "Whoever is on the side of Israel, let everyone know that we are against them."[12] Erdoğan champions the cause of the Palestinians and is a vocal critic of Israel at every turn.[13]

In addition to the developments within Turkey, Turkish ties with Iran and Russia are strengthening in many areas, but especially in their cooperation in Syria.[14] Turkey has invaded northern Syria with Russian approval. It has deployed troops to Libya. Turkey has encroached into Iraq, casting a large shadow over the Kurdish people who reside there. It is flexing its muscles in what some believe is an attempt to revive the Ottoman Empire. The growing association of this trio—Russia, Iran, and Syria—that appears so prominently in Ezekiel 38 strikingly foreshadows Ezekiel's prophecy.

The prominence of Turkey in Ezekiel 38 also highlights an interesting twist. The Quran contains its own version of the Battle of Gog and Magog, which it calls the War of Yajuj and Majuj (18:96; 21:96) and which involves Turkey. The Quranic version was written about a thousand years after Ezekiel prophesied and teaches that Gog and Magog were two bands of Turks that spread corruption through the earth during the time of Abraham. They were eventually imprisoned behind a great barrier to restrain their activity. Throughout the centuries they tried to escape without success. When Allah issues his decree in the end times, the barrier will collapse, and Gog and Magog will rush out in all directions, pouring into the land of Israel to attack Muslims living there. Allah will wipe them out in response to the prayers of Jesus, using a terrible, deadly disease or plague. This language was clearly borrowed from Ezekiel 38:22, and adapted to fit a totally different narrative and outcome.

THE END-TIME COALITION AGAINST ISRAEL

Rosh (ancient Rashu, Rasapu, Ros, and Rus)	Russia
Magog (ancient Scythians)	Central Asia
Meshech (ancient Muschki and Musku)	Turkey
Tubal (ancient Tubalu)	Turkey
Persia	Iran
Ethiopia (Cush)	Sudan
Put or Phut	Libya

| Gomer (ancient Cimmerians) | Turkey |
| Beth-togarmah (ancient Til-garimmu or Tegarma) | Turkey |

The nations in this list are all enemies or at least not friends with Israel. They all have the desire at one level or another to get rid of Israel. To varying degrees, they are either forming or strengthening their ties to one another. They all appear regularly in the headlines, some almost every day. No great leap is necessary to imagine these nations colluding together to overrun Israel in the near future, especially if Israel launches a preemptive military strike against Iran.

Three of the key players—Russia, Turkey, and Iran—are working together in Syria to blunt American influence and entrench themselves on Israel's northern border.[15]

Ezekiel's list of the participants in his last-days invasion ends with the words "many peoples with you" (Ezekiel 38:6). This catch-all phrase could indicate that more nations, not specifically listed, will join the war against Israel. Ezekiel lists Israel's distant or far enemies in every direction. North is Russia, east is Iran, south is Sudan, and west is Libya. By listing these far enemies, Ezekiel may be including the inner ring of nations around Israel as well, nations or territories such as Syria, Jordan, Egypt, Lebanon, Iraq, and Gaza.

Whatever measure you use, the ingredients for the Gog coalition seem to be coming together. All that's required to finish the process is a catalyst. The showdown between Iran and Israel could easily be the trigger that sets the final movements in motion.

THE OPPOSITION

Everything we see today suggests that Iran and the other nations in Ezekiel 38 are on a collision course with Israel and would gladly join the Gog alliance when it comes together.

Nevertheless, the Middle East is a complicated place. Iran has many enemies, even among Muslims, who fear her and would do anything to neutralize her power and influence. In the current climate, we would expect many nations to steer clear of any Iranian war with Israel and even root for an Iranian defeat. Iranian cruise missiles and drones struck the Aramco oil facility in Saudi Arabia in 2019 shutting down half of Saudi Arabia's oil production. Iran and Saudi Arabia came perilously close to war. Saudi Arabia strongly opposes Iranian aggression.

Ezekiel 38 corresponds to what we see today, both in the nations that are part of the coalition against Israel as well as those who oppose it. The specificity of this prophecy is astounding. Ezekiel presents the nations in the Gog coalition that will join Russia and Iran against Israel and also lays out the nations that will object to the invasion, albeit lamely. Amazingly, this assembly of nations that sits on the sidelines and lodges its protest is just as perfectly aligned as the aggressors.

> "Thus says the Lord God, 'It will come about on that day,
> that thoughts will come into your mind and you will devise
> an evil plan, and you will say, "I will go up against the

land of unwalled villages. I will go against those who are at rest, that live securely, all of them living without walls and having no bars or gates, to capture spoil and to seize plunder, to turn your hand against the waste places which are *now* inhabited, and against the people who are gathered from the nations, who have acquired cattle and goods, who live at the center of the world." Sheba and Dedan and the merchants of Tarshish with all its villages will say to you, "Have you come to capture spoil? Have you assembled your company to seize plunder, to carry away silver and gold, to take away cattle and goods, to capture great spoil?"'" (Ezekiel 38:10–13)

Who are the nations who lodge their protest to the Iranian invasion of Israel?

Sheba and Dedan

The first protesting nations are identified as, "Sheba and Dedan and the merchants of Tarshish with all its villages." Sheba and Dedan are easy to locate. They're the nations we know today as Saudi Arabia and the more moderate Gulf States. These Sunni Muslim nations are vehemently opposed to Iran and its nuclear quest.

What we see today lines up seamlessly with Ezekiel's prophecy. It requires no active imagination to envision these nations opposing Iran's actions, yet standing on the sidelines, taking a knee, and offering no more than verbal dissent when the Gog invasion erupts.

Merchants of Tarshish

The reference to "the merchants of Tarshish with all its villages" poses a greater challenge to identify. Even English translations differ somewhat.

English Standard Version	"the merchants of Tarshish and all its leaders"
King James Version	"the merchants of Tarshish, with all the young lions thereof"
New Living Translation	"the merchants of Tarshish"
New International Version	"the merchants of Tarshish and all her villages"

Three ancient locations were identified as "Tarshish."[16] The most accepted view is that Tarshish was a wealthy, flourishing Phoenician colony situated in modern Spain. This outpost was renowned for exporting silver, iron, tin, and lead (Jeremiah 10:9; Ezekiel 27:12, 25).

The words "and all its leaders" (ESV) or "the young lions thereof" (KJV) seem to refer to powerful, energetic rulers who will join with Tarshish to verbally oppose Gog's invasion. These leaders will evidently walk in lockstep with Tarshish. Tarshish is often associated in Scripture with the far West. When the prophet Jonah wanted to go as far away from Nineveh as possible, he headed to Tarshish (Jonah 1:1–3). Since Tarshish, located in

Spain, was the farthest western location known in that day, I believe "Tarshish and all its leaders" is a reference to the Western powers or Western world in the end times who will join the moderate Arab states in denouncing the invasion of Israel.[17]

The mention of Western powers brings up the possibility the United States is included in this group of protesting nations. While there's no way to make this connection with any certainty, it remains a realistic possibility. Nevertheless, even if this is a veiled reference to America, it provides almost no helpful insight into any activities by the United States other than a weak protest against the Russian-Islamic invasion of Israel. So, either way, it's not really significant. We'll discuss possible biblical identifications of the United States further in chapter 8.

INTENSIFYING INTERSECTION

As you can see, the scenario presented in Ezekiel 38 mirrors the present world political situation. Russia continues to expand its footprint in the Middle East, forging and fortifying partnerships with Iran, Turkey, Syria, and other Arab nations. The Islamic nations that correspond to ancient Magog (central Asia) are developing and deepening ties with Iran, Russia, and Turkey. Hatred for Israel in Iran and other Muslim nations in the region continues to seethe. It's easy to picture the alliance Ezekiel describes pouring into Israel in an all-out attempt to wipe Israel off the face of the earth. Likewise, in the current climate, it's not too difficult to imagine the moderate Gulf States and Western democracies raising loud protest and objection to the invasion but opting to stand on the sidelines and watch the whole matter unfold.

Ezekiel's prophecy reads like today's headlines. Current events are intersecting with biblical prophecy at a quickening pace. All that's left is for something to set it all in motion.

We can't be sure what the trigger will be, but the mounting showdown with Iran is looking more and more likely as a candidate. I appreciate Joel Rosenberg's admonition in light of Ezekiel 38–39.

What then are we to make of all this? It is almost as if the Lord has perfectly allowed world circumstances to conform in more than one way, giving us multiple possibilities to fulfill Ezekiel's prophecy. Is Gog emerging in front of us? We may find out very soon. One thing is clear however; the Lord wants us all to remain alert and on our knees.[18]

Amen!

CHAPTER 6

FINAL SHOWDOWN: THE WAR OF GOG AND MAGOG

This war will be a war unlike any we have seen thus far in history.
—Dr. Walter C. Kaiser Jr., *Preaching and Teaching the Last Things*

In 2019 my wife and I and another couple had the privilege of visiting Normandy, France, on June 5, the day before the seventy-fifth anniversary of the D-Day invasion. We hired a van and a driver for the day and drove up from Paris. The entire region was filled with reenactors dressed in uniforms from World War II. Tanks, trucks, jeeps, and cannons were on display everywhere. World War II–era airplanes were humming overhead. We made several stops in the area, but the most important, moving site was Omaha Beach. The Normandy American Cemetery and Memorial is located on a beautiful bluff overlooking Omaha Beach. Almost ten thousand crosses line the landscape.

The most special aspect of the trip was seeing the aged veterans who had taken part in the invasion return for one final act of remembrance. I'll never forget meeting them and hearing their harrowing stories. They were applauded everywhere they went and received much deserved appreciation. Waiting in the airport for our return home from Paris, my wife and I sat next to two venerable gentlemen who had hit the beaches to free a continent. On our flight home, another survivor of the Normandy invasion sat across us. Spending time with these heroes was better than any history lesson one could imagine.

The invasion in June 1944 was officially known as Operation Overlord, but the popular name is D-Day. According to CNN, "The 'D' stands for Day. D-Day is code for the day an important military attack is scheduled to begin."[1]

After a great deal of strategizing and planning, D-Day was finally scheduled by General Dwight Eisenhower for June 6, 1944. As we've seen, God has a D-Day scheduled on His prophetic calendar—a day when an important military attack will begin that will ultimately bring great victory and triumph for God and His people. This end-time D-Day is the Battle of

Gog and Magog. The key actors are moving into place for its commencement. Chief among them is Iran.

But what will happen on this D-Day when Iran and its allies launch their all-out invasion of Israel? How will the showdown with Iran culminate? Where's it all headed? Ezekiel graphically describes what happens before, during, and after the battle.

BEFORE THE BATTLE: THE AIM

While many of the details of the final showdown with Iran are shrouded in mystery, the one thing we can know for sure is that this invasion will occur. It's already scheduled on God's prophetic calendar. While there's much we can't know, we do know the nations that will join this invasion. Ezekiel specifically identifies them, as we've already seen.

Ezekiel also provides some of the reasons or motivations for this attack. He clearly states their aim in their aggression against Israel. Several reasons for this invasion can be discerned from the text and related passages.

To Capture the Wealth of Israel

The exact nature of the wealth in Ezekiel 38:11–12 is never specifically stated; however, recent discoveries of vast oil and gas reserves in Israel are one possible answer. Several gargantuan natural gas deposits and shale oil sites have been discovered in various locations.

To Command the Middle East

Taking out Israel would give Iran and the other Islamic nations their greatest victory and prize and pave the way for their long past empire to be reestablished.

To Conquer Israel

Every Muslim nation covets the reality of driving Israel into the sea. Ezekiel says these invaders will "come like a storm" and "like a cloud covering the land" (38:9). This sounds like a desire to overwhelm and overrun Israel, leaving nothing behind but ruin.

To Contest the Antichrist

Assuming this invasion occurs during the first half of the coming seven-year Tribulation, as I believe, Israel will be enjoying her peace treaty with Antichrist when this attack occurs. Therefore, an attack against Israel would at the same time represent a direct confrontation against the Antichrist. The invasion of Israel will be an open challenge to the West and its leader, the Antichrist, by Russia and its Islamic allies. Parallel prophecies in Daniel 9:27 and 11:41–44 tell us that at the midpoint of the seven-year Tribulation, the Antichrist will break his covenant with Israel and invade the land himself. Obviously, the total annihilation of the Russian-Islamic forces will leave a gaping power vacuum. The Antichrist will seize this opportunity to fill that void and consolidate his power. This will lead to the establishment of his one world religion, government, and economy, which will dominate the world for the final three and a half years of the end times, just before the return of Christ.

To Counter the Rebuilding of the Jewish Temple

During the first half of the seven-year Tribulation, Israel will rebuild its temple (Daniel 9:27; Matthew 24:15; 2 Thessalonians 2:4). It could be that Iran and these allies invade Israel to protect the Dome of the Rock and the Al-Aqṣā mosque that stand on the Temple Mount. The entire thirty-five-acre area that the Jews call the Temple Mount is known by Muslims as al-Haram ash-Sharif, or the Noble Sanctuary. Any attempt by the Jewish people to rebuild their temple could set off this furious attack by the Muslim world supported by Russia.

DURING THE BATTLE: THE AVALANCHE

After the preparations for the battle are completed, the enemy armies will swoop into the unsuspecting nation of Israel living in peace and prosperity. Ezekiel describes the invading flood in vivid terms, saying the armies will come "like a storm and cover the land like a cloud" (38:9). The battle and its outcome are presented in devastating detail.

When these nations invade the land of Israel, it will look like the most one-sided mismatch in history. The odds will be overwhelmingly in favor of the invaders. The world will look on in stunned fear as it appears Israel is about to be annihilated. The armies will gather and pour into the land like an invading swarm of locusts. From all appearances, Israel is finished. But just when it looks as though all is lost, God will dramatically intervene on behalf of Israel. He will descend in His fury to destroy the would-be conquerors: "But this is what the Sovereign LORD says: When Gog invades the land of Israel, my fury will boil over!" (Ezekiel 38:18 NLT).

The battle of Gog and Magog will be the greatest turn-around in history. The tables will turn in a flash—from Israel's certain destruction to absolute triumph. God will come down to deliver Israel. Dr. Walter Kaiser Jr., quoted at the beginning of this chapter, says that "God, for his own name's sake, will sensationally rescue Israel when all other sources of help fail."[2]

Of course, God could just speak the word and the armies would melt before Him, but in this battle, He will employ four disasters to destroy the invading horde.

1. A Devastating Earthquake (Ezekiel 38:19–20)

The earthquake will be cataclysmic.

> "In My zeal and in My blazing wrath I declare that on that day there will surely be a great earthquake in the land of Israel. The fish of the sea, the birds of the heavens, the beasts of the field, all the creeping things that creep on the earth, and all the men who are on the face of the earth will shake at My presence; the mountains also will be thrown down, the steep pathways will collapse and every wall will fall to the ground."

2. Deadly Infighting Among the Invading Army (38:21)

In the chaos that ensues from the rattling earthquake, the invasion force will be thrown into confusion and will turn against itself. The soldiers will kill anyone in sight. When the dust settles, this will be the biggest incident of death by friendly fire in military history.

3. Dreadful Disease (38:22)

An outbreak of incurable, lethal plagues will kill people instantly.

4. Driving Rain, Hailstones, Fire, and Burning Sulphur (38:22)

The battle of Gog and Magog won't last long. When God steps in, the destruction will be swift and sobering. Smoldering heaps of weapons will litter the land. Carnage will cover the country.

Dr. Walter Kaiser summarizes the catastrophic defeat:

> But things will not end well for the nations that press their attack against Israel, for in the end, what they are doing is nothing less than an attack on God and his plan for time and eternity. In one great push, an axis of nations from that part of the world will make one huge incursion into the land of Israel, but that will call for the response of God himself. The carnage, bloodshed and loss of life and power will be unrivaled up to that point in history. This will be at once

one of the darkest, and yet also one of the brightest, days of all history, as God settles the issue in a startling way. Such is the predicted fortunes of the War of Gog and Magog against Israel in the end of the days of history's ongoing time line.[3]

Collateral Damage

As crushing as the defeat will be for the invaders, it won't end in the land of Israel. Ezekiel says that the firestorms of God's judgment will extend even to the homeland of some of the invading nations. "And I will send fire upon Magog and those who inhabit the coastlands in safety; and they will know that I am the LORD" (Ezekiel 39:6).

Commenting on this verse, Joel Rosenberg said:

This suggests that targets throughout Russia and the former Soviet Union, as well as Russia's allies, will be supernaturally struck on this day of judgment and partially or completely consumed. These could be limited to nuclear missile silos, military bases, radar installations, defense ministries, intelligence headquarters, and other government buildings of various kinds. But such targets could very well also include religious centers, such as mosques, madrassas, Islamic schools and universities, and other facilities that preach hatred against Jews and Christians and call for the destruction of Israel. Either way, we will have to expect extensive collateral damage, and many civilians will be at severe risk.[4]

The extent of this collateral damage is not stated, but we can be sure it will send a strong message of God's displeasure with the actions of these nations as well as evidence of His sovereign might.

Chronological Decision

One important issue about this coming war is its timing. When does this invasion fit on God's prophetic calendar? The chronology of this invasion has been related to about every point in the end times. Some believe it could transpire at any time, and that the invasion will precede the rapture or at least the Tribulation.[5] Others believe Ezekiel 38 is another description of the final Battle of Armageddon.[6] Still others equate it with the reference to Gog and Magog in Revelation 20:8.[7]

In an effort not to get too far in the weeds, I won't present the pros and cons of all the views in detail, but I do want to briefly consider several internal markers that help us locate this invasion on the end-time schedule of events.

First, the Jewish people must be regathered to their ancient homeland. Ezekiel 37 is the prophetic prelude to the invasion in Ezekiel 38, and it prophesies the end-time regathering of the Jewish people to the land of Israel. Clearly the Jewish people in the nation of Israel cannot be invaded if the nation doesn't exist. The regathering and restoration of the Jewish people beginning in the 1940s was a key event that set many other prophecies in motion. As John Walvoord noted, "Ezekiel's prophecy obviously could not have been fulfilled prior to 1945, for the nation of Israel was not regathered to her ancient land. Until recently Israel's situation did not correspond to that which is described in Ezekiel's passage. Ezekiel's prophecy of twenty-five hundred years ago seems to have anticipated the return of Israel to their ancient land as a prelude to the climax of the present age."[8] Israel's presence in the land is the first major precondition that must be in place for this war to begin.

Second, the invasion will happen in the "last days" or "latter years" of Israel's history. This narrows the timing and setting of the invasion to the end times, but more specifically after the rapture of the church to heaven. Only then will the latter years for Israel begin.

Third, Ezekiel prophesies that Iran and her allies will come against Israel "after many days" at a time when the people of Israel are living in relative peace and prosperity (38:8–12). Ezekiel repeatedly emphasizes that when this invasion occurs, Israel will be back in the land, "living securely" (38:8, 11, 14) and "at rest" (38:11). That hardly describes what we see in Israel today. The land is prosperous but not at peace or at rest. Israelis live in a constant state of high alert. But according to Scripture, a time is coming when Israel will enjoy a season of peace. This will come about when Israel enters into a covenant or treaty with the coming Western leader, who will be the final Antichrist (Daniel 9:27). Under this treaty he will guarantee Israel peace and security. Therefore, for this invasion to occur, Israel must be present in the land, prosperous, and peaceful.

Taking all these internal markers into consideration, I believe this battle will occur during the first half of the coming seven-year Tribulation, when Israel will be living under her peace treaty with Antichrist. Pastor and evangelical author David Jeremiah agrees: "Thus, we have the time of the . . . invasion of Israel pinpointed. To summarize, it will come after Israel returns to this homeland, after it has become highly prosperous, and after the implementation of the seven-year peace treaty with the Antichrist."[9]

The late John Walvoord held the same view of the timing of this battle. "There is only one period in the future that clearly fits this description of Ezekiel," he wrote, "and that is the first half of Daniel's seventieth week of God's program for Israel (Daniel 9:27)."[10] He continues: "Under that covenant, Israel will be able to relax, for their Gentile enemies will have become their friends, apparently guaranteeing their borders and promising them freedom. During that first three and one-half years, we have the one time when regathered Israel is at rest and secure."[11]

The buildup we see today indicates that the coming of Christ to rapture His people to heaven could be very soon, setting in motion the cascade of events that will bring about the Battle of Gog and Magog.

AFTER THE BATTLE

Three main events unfold in the aftermath of the battle.

1. The Call to the Feast (Ezekiel 39:4–5, 17–20)

The aftermath of the battle is a grisly, gruesome scene. The carnage that results from this slaughter will provide a great feast for the birds of the air and the beasts of the field. God refers to the carnage as His "sacrificial feast" (39:17 ESV) and His "banquet table" (39:20 NLT), to which He invites the birds and the beasts as His guests.

> "As for you, son of man, thus says the Lord GOD, 'Speak to every kind of bird and to every beast of the field, "Assemble and come, gather from every side to My sacrifice which I am going to sacrifice for you, as a great sacrifice on the mountains of Israel, that you may eat flesh and drink blood. You will eat the flesh of mighty men and drink the blood of the princes of the earth, as though they were rams, lambs, goats and bulls, all of them fatlings of Bashan. So you will eat fat until you are glutted, and drink blood until you are drunk, from My sacrifice which I have sacrificed for you. You will be glutted at My table with horses and charioteers, with mighty men and all the men of war," declares the Lord GOD. (Ezekiel 39:17–20)

A similar banquet will be held after the Battle of Armageddon at the end of the Tribulation (Revelation 19:17–21).

2. The Cleansing of the Land (Ezekiel 39:11–12, 14–16)

The cleansing of the land entails two stages. First, sanitation squads will comb the countryside for seven months after the battle. Not all the bodies can be buried quickly, and the bones will be left behind. These clean-up teams will set up markers wherever they see a human bone. The gravediggers coming behind them will see the markers and remove the remains to the valley of Hamon-Gog, which means "Gog's hordes," for burial. The cleansing efforts will be so widespread that a town will be constructed in the valley near the gravesites to aid those who are cleansing the land. The name of the town will be *Hamonah* (horde). Concerning the burial of these invading armies, Warren Wiersbe said, "They arrogantly entered Israel as proud soldiers but would be buried like slaughtered animals."[12]

The second phase of cleansing the land will involve burning the leftover weapons for seven years (Ezekiel 39:9–10). In describing the weapons used during this invasion, Ezekiel refers to "shields and bucklers, bows and arrows, war clubs and spears" (39:9). Ezekiel mentions horses as the means of transportation for the invading army (38:4, 15). Some believe the devastation during the future time of the Tribulation, possibly from the use of nuclear weapons, will be so severe that armies will regress to using ancient weapons and riding on horses.

It is said that in 1947 Albert Einstein was asked at a dinner party what new weapons he believed might be employed in World War III. After a long pause, he allegedly responded, "I don't know what weapons might be used in World War III. But there isn't any doubt what weapons will be used in World War IV . . . stone spears."[13]

While that scenario is certainly possible, I believe we should understand Ezekiel's language as referring to contemporary equivalents such as tanks, rifles, and modern artillery; otherwise it would have had no meaning for the people living in Ezekiel's day. We should view these weapons the same way we interpret the nations in Ezekiel 38. We look for the modern counterparts of Rosh, Gomer, Persia, and so on, since the ancient names are no longer relevant.

Since the battle of Gog and Magog occurs during the first half of the Tribulation, the Israelites will continue to burn these weapons for the remainder of the seven-year Tribulation and for a brief time on into the millennial kingdom that will follow.

3. The Confirmation of the Lord (Ezekiel 39:6–7)

As He unleashes His wrath and fury, God will graciously pour out His mercy. He will use the awesome display of His holiness and greatness against the invading armies not only to protect His people but also to bring many to salvation, both from the nations and from Israel.

> "I will bring you against My land, so that the nations may know Me when I am sanctified through you before their eyes, O Gog. . . . I will magnify Myself, sanctify Myself, and make Myself known in the sight of many nations; and they will know that I am the LORD. . . . And I will send fire upon Magog and those who inhabit the coastlands in safety; and they will know that I am the LORD. My holy name I will make known in the midst of My people Israel;

and I will not let My holy name be profaned anymore. And the nations will know that I am the LORD, the Holy One in Israel. . . . And I will set My glory among the nations . . . . And the house of Israel will know that I am the LORD their God from that day onward." (Ezekiel 38:16, 23; 39:6, 7, 21, 22)

Charles Ryrie, in *The Ryrie Study Bible*, notes, "The twofold purpose of this judgment is that the nations might acknowledge God's glory and that Israel might know God's grace."[14]

It's often true that times of disaster and even judgment can bring people to their senses. Judgment serves as a sobering wake-up call. While I don't believe 9/11 was necessarily an act of divine judgment against America, it was a terrible display of violence. In its aftermath Americans packed churches and cried out to God. While people all too quickly went back to sleep, there was at least a brief, intense time of awareness and awakening.

The result of God's judgment in Ezekiel 38–39 will be similar, yet real and lasting. Still, even people from those nations that have come against God and Israel will have an opportunity to acknowledge the greatness and grace of God and be delivered from their sins. Old Testament scholar Christopher J. H. Wright reminds us, "As God's redeemed people we cannot contemplate the ultimate defeat of evil and the destruction of the wicked with any sense of moral superiority. For we know that apart from the grace of God which has brought us to repentance and restoration, the same fate would justly await us."[15]

CONCLUSIONS

There are numerous conclusions to draw from Ezekiel 38–39, but here are a few for you to gather your thoughts around.

- An axis of nations that surround Israel—the far enemies or outer ring of nations—will conspire and come against Israel in the latter years to get rid of Israel once and for all. We see this alliance merging today.

- The invasion of Israel will be a surprise attack, occurring during the first half of the seven-year Tribulation, when Israel is living in peace and prosperity under a coming peace treaty that will be forged by the Antichrist. The number one issue in the Middle East today is the yearning for peace between Israel, the Palestinians, and Israel's other near neighbors.

- When Israel is invaded and it appears that she is finished, God will dramatically intervene to destroy the avalanche of allies and will even send shock waves of judgment against the homeland of the invaders.

- God's demonstration of power and greatness will be so overwhelming that the nations will be forced to acknowledge that He alone is the true God.

- The people of Israel will begin to recognize there is no one like their God and will experience a turning to the Lord.

- God is sovereign. He controls nations and nature. No one can stand against Him.

- God is the only Savior. He is the only One who can deliver nations and individuals.
- Salvation is found in no one else. Turning to Him and trusting in Him is your only hope. Jesus is coming for those who have come to Him.

CHAPTER 7

ISRAEL AND IRAN AT WAR

*Opposition to and vilification of the Jewish
state is ingrained in modern Iran's DNA.*
—Timothy Furnish, *The Stream*

*Iran has encircled Israel from all four sides.
Nothing will be left of Israel.*
—Abbas Nilforoushan, deputy
commander of operations of the Iranian
Revolutionary Guard Corps

Scripture shines its prophetic spotlight squarely on the Middle East. This region, especially Israel, is ground zero for the end times. If we want to know where we are on God's prophetic clock, Israel is God's timepiece.

The late pastor Adrian Rogers summed up Israel's place in God's prophetic program:

> These are dangerous days in which we live! The storm clouds are gathering. The lightning is flashing—and the lightning rod is Israel. Christians cannot deny or ignore the significance of the nation of Israel . . . The eyes of the entire world are upon the tiny state of Israel, and your eyes need to be there too, because the Jews and Israel are the people and the land of destiny. As the Jew goes, so goes the world. Israel is God's yardstick. Israel is God's measuring rod. Israel is God's blueprint. Israel is God's program for what He is doing in the world.[1]

Charles H. Dyer, an expert in Middle Eastern history and geography, wrote, "God gave Israel a starring role in His drama of the ages, and Israel will again take center stage in the final act. You cannot understand the future without understanding the part assigned to Israel."[2] Israel is mentioned more than twenty-five hundred times in the Bible. After almost two thousand years of dispersion to more than seventy countries, the modern state of Israel was founded and formed in 1948. The Jewish people are still in the process of being regathered to their ancient homeland.

Their regathering to their land has set off a firestorm in the Middle East. Israel is surrounded by enemies who want her driven into the sea. The animosity of the nations against Israel that will prevail in the end times was prophesied by Zechariah about five hundred years before the coming of Christ.

> The burden of the word of the LORD concerning Israel. Thus declares the LORD who stretches out the heavens, lays the foundation of the earth, and forms the spirit of man within him, "Behold, I am going to make Jerusalem a cup that causes reeling to all the peoples around; and when the siege is against Jerusalem, it will also be against Judah. It will come about in that day that I will make Jerusalem a heavy stone for all the peoples; all who lift it will be severely injured. And all the nations of the earth will be gathered against it." (Zechariah 12:1–3)

What's happening in Israel today bears a remarkable correspondence to this ancient prophecy but even more specifically to the war in Ezekiel 38–39. Israel is at war. She has been at war with Iran since the Islamic Revolution in 1979.

Iran's mullah regime detests Israel. So do Iran's elite military units. This was evidenced at a recent graduation ceremony of Iranian officers of the Revolutionary Guard Academy. During the ceremony Iranian officers had an Israeli flag painted on the bottom of their boots that could be seen clearly as they goose-stepped like Nazi troops of the 1930s. Iran wants to put its boot on Israel's neck. The obsession of every Iranian soldier is the subjugation of Israel under the heel of Iranian power. Speaking of Israel, a top Iranian general in charge of

Iran's Revolutionary Guards said, "This sinister regime must be wiped off the map and this is no longer a dream but it is an achievable goal."[3]

Iran's premier clandestine military unit, which functions under Iran's Revolutionary Guard is called the Quds Force. The Arabic name for Jerusalem is Al Quds. This name was selected to be a constant reminder of Iran's relentless desire to recapture Jerusalem and put it under Shiite control. All of this fits the prophecy of Ezekiel 38 to a tee.

THE SHADOW WAR

In response to Iranian hatred and aggression, Israel has engaged in a long-term shadow war with Iran to neutralize the potential threat. Israel has carried out numerous very effective cyber-attacks against Iran's nuclear megaplex. She has also assassinated a host of Iranian nuclear scientists to slow Iran's progress toward the nuclear finish line. Israel is taking every step short of all-out war to stem the tide of Iran's aggression.

Nemesis from the North

Another key element to the shadow war with Israel is Iran's numerous surrogates that they employ to deflect the focus from themselves. Iran has forged and armed a powerful network of proxies that are able to attack Israel in different ways and from all sides. Iran's deputy chief of staff of the Iranian armed forces has bragged, "Our defensive depth has stretched to the

Mediterranean Sea and our front has extended to the borders of the Zionist regime [of Israel]."[4]

Dore Gold, Israel's former ambassador to the United Nations, has noted, "Tehran is determined to take the Shia forces from around the Middle East and deploy them in Syria—first and foremost against Israel's north, but with implications for stability in Jordan, Saudi Arabia, and the rest of the Arabian Peninsula."[5]

Israel is at war with Iran's main proxy in Lebanon, Hezbollah, the nemesis from the north. *Hezbollah* means "Party of God." It was founded in the early 1980s. Hezbollah carries out Iran's bidding.

Israel and Hezbollah squared off in a bloody, brutal, month-long war in 2006 and haven't really stopped fighting since. In the meantime, Hezbollah has created more sophisticated launching sites and expanded its deadly arsenal. Hezbollah is a ferocious, formidable foe that sits on the Israel's northern doorstep, waiting to pounce whenever Iran gives the signal.

In addition to Hezbollah in the north, Iranian-recruited militants from Afghanistan are active near the Golan Heights of Israel, claiming that they have come to fight the "Zionists."

Their final target, they state, is Israel. They are living and training in Syria.[6]

Strife in the South

Iran also controls Israel's foe to the south, Palestinian Islamic Jihad in Gaza. They, too, stand ready and eager to do Iran's bidding. As they await their orders for an all-out attack, they act as constant agitator, firing rockets into southern Israel to inflict as much damage as possible.

The growing crisis shows no signs of slowing. Iran is embedding itself in Syria. Hezbollah is entrenching and hardening in Lebanon. Palestinian Islamic Jihad (PIJ) is thriving in Gaza. Israel is working to prevent or at least impede these ongoing threats. That's the current showdown in a nutshell. Israel will keep striking Iranian assets in Syria to deliver temporary setbacks and continue its cat-and-mouse game with Hezbollah. Israel will continue to hold PIJ at bay. But eventually Iran and Hezbollah won't take it anymore, and ultimately Israel will reach a point where more force is required. Those scenarios can come about separately or simultaneously. In either case, war will break out, possibly engulfing the region.

"What are the implications for Israel?" asks *Haaretz*'s Amos Harel. Yaakov Amidror, Netanyahu's former national security adviser, responds: "High probability of more Iranian aggression and even broader conflict with Israel if, in the latter half of 2020, Iran ramps up uranium enrichment. Israel must be ready to tackle Iran on its own." Amidror's forecast for northern Israel is no rosier. Harel reports: "Israel must be ready for escalation, including preemptive warfare with Hezbollah."[7]

Everyone yearns for a diplomatic solution to the showdown. A quote attributed to Winston Churchill is that "jaw-jaw is better than war-war." Everyone agrees that talking is generally better than fighting. But how can Israel "jaw-jaw" with an enemy that constantly chants "death to Israel," calls it a "cancerous tumor," and yearns for the day the Jewish state is eradicated? Iran regularly threatens to "wipe Israel off the map" and says that "Israel will disappear." It is working to strengthen its grip on Lebanon, Syria, Iraq, Yemen, and the Gaza Strip. Iran has deployed missiles in Yemen that could reach Israel. Iran's tentacles now span the entire Middle East. Most importantly, and most dangerously, Iran is now poised and perched on Israel's border in Syria.

MORE THAN MEETS THE EYE

Iranian efforts to annihilate Israel are occurring against the dark backdrop of increasing anti-Semitism. Hatred for Israel today is present in its most concentrated form in Iran, but anti-Semitism is increasing at an alarming rate worldwide. We all see it. Synagogues are regularly the scenes of ruthless slaughter. It's open season on the Jewish people. The resurgence of rage against Israel is palpable.

Sadly, this is nothing new. Anti-Semitism is as old as Abraham. Through the millennia, there have been numerous attempts to wipe out the Jews. The Jewish people have been the victims of age-long persecution and pogroms to exterminate their race. But the recent increase in anti-Semitism is striking.

Have you ever wondered why there is so much pent-up hatred for the Jewish people and the state of Israel? Why won't it go away? Why has it persisted for so long? While persecutors of the Jewish people down through the ages have had their own evil justifications for their actions, there are two main underlying reasons behind the hatred of Israel and desire to drive them out of their land.

First, and more specifically, the clash between the Jewish people and their neighbors goes back four thousand years to the days of Abraham and his two sons. The central issue is: Who owns the land? According to Genesis 12:1–3 and 15:15–21, God made an eternal covenant with Abraham giving him the promised land. The borders of the land are carefully outlined in Genesis 15:18–21. The covenant blessings and land promise were transferred to Abraham's son Isaac, not Ishmael. Centuries later, when Islam came along, the story was changed to highlight Ishmael in place of Isaac.

Muslims believe Abraham took Ishmael to Mount Moriah instead of Isaac (Genesis 22). They maintain that Abraham and Hagar fled to Mecca with Ishmael where he became a prophet and an ancestor to Muhammad. The Bible is clear that God blessed Ishmael. "As for Ishmael, I have heard you; behold, I will bless him, and will make him fruitful and will multiply him exceedingly. He shall become the father of twelve princes, and I will make him a great nation" (Genesis 17:20).

Nevertheless, the promised land was deeded by God forever to Abraham and then to Isaac and then to Isaac's son Jacob and his descendants. The Jewish people own the land, the city of Jerusalem, and the Temple Mount, according to the Bible. Yet, Muslims believe it belongs to them. Therein lies the historical rivalry and hostility.

Iranians are not descendants of Ishmael; they are Persians. Some Arabs today are not descendants of Ishmael, but many are. Regardless, followers of Islam believe the land is theirs by divine right. The battle for the land of Israel we see today stems from this ancient rivalry four millennia in the making.

Second, the primary driving force behind anti-Semitism in general is the Devil, God's enemy, Satan. Satan is anti-Christ and anti-Semitic. He hates Jesus, and he hates the Jewish people because God has a purpose and plan for the Jewish people in the end of days. God promised the Jewish people a specific piece of real estate in the Middle East in Genesis 15:18–21, and He gave it to them as their possession forever.

Jesus is coming back someday to fulfill that promise to Israel. He will bring the Jewish people into their promised land under His rule.

God also promised that a Messiah from the line of King David would rule over Israel in their land. To prevent the fulfillment of that prophecy, Satan worked throughout the Old Testament to wipe out the Jewish people and specifically the line of David to keep Jesus from being born. When that failed, he tempted Jesus to sin, to disqualify Him from being the Savior (Matthew 4). When he was unsuccessful in that ploy, Satan moved the Jewish leaders and the Romans to kill Him. But Jesus came back to life on the third day (Matthew 27–28).

Satan's last-ditch effort to derail God's program and defeat God's promises to Abraham and David is to eliminate the Jewish people. In so doing, Satan can thwart the promises of God. He can prevent Jesus from ruling over the Jewish people as promised. This explains the irrational hatred Israel's neighbors have for the Jewish state and the Jewish people. They are driven by a demonically inspired detestation of Israel.

Make no mistake. Satan is the world's greatest anti-Semite. That explains the dark agenda against Israel and the gathering storm in the Middle East. It explains why events are building in the Middle East to a grand climax. And it explains Iran's obsession with eliminating Israel from the map and its expanding plan to encircle Israel with its proxies in a ring of fire.

Israel continues to lash out against the encroachment and entrenchment of Iranian power. Israeli jets have flown a thousand sorties into Lebanon, Syria, and Iraq to stop the slow tightening of the noose around its neck. Yet time seems to be running out. Some larger, more destructive strikes will be necessary, assuring fierce retaliation and revenge from Iran.

Israeli counterterrorism expert Professor Boaz Ganor said, "We are very close to a war. . . . I really don't remember a more fragile, dangerous time . . . If this war will start, it will be an unprecedented war in the Middle East and Israel." He then pointed out that in such a war, "Israel's Iron Dome would be swarmed with three thousand rockets per day. Once you understand the threat in that way, you understand the number of casualties and the level of damage and destruction that Israel will face."[8]

Even the conflict between the United States and Iran could quickly expand to include Israel. Mojtaba Zolnour, the chairman of the Iranian parliament's National Security and Foreign Policy Committee, said, "If the US attacks us, only half an hour will remain of Israel's lifespan."[9] Whatever happens, Israel will bear the brunt. Iran will leverage any opportunity to inflict damage on Israel.

FUTURE TENSE

The Israel-Iran war is here. All that remains is the opening salvo that will set events in motion. Michael Oren, former Israeli ambassador to the United States, gives this sobering analysis:

> Israel is girding for the worst and acting on the assumption that fighting could break out at any time. And it's not hard to imagine how it might arrive. The conflagration, like so many in the Middle East, could be ignited by a single spark. Israeli fighter jets have already conducted hundreds of bombing raids against Iranian targets in Lebanon, Syria, and Iraq. . . . The result could be a counterstrike by Iran, using cruise missiles that penetrate Israel's air defenses and smash into targets like the Kiryah, Tel Aviv's equivalent of the Pentagon. . . . And then, after a day of large-scale exchanges, the real war would begin.[10]

Yaakov Katz, editor-in-chief of the *Jerusalem Post*, envisions how the war could start.

> The missiles will come in low, after being in the air for almost an hour, and when they hit, they will be coming just over the horizon. People who witness the attack will remember later that the missiles didn't fall from the sky. They flew at their target straight, like a bullet.
>
> The drones will hit just a few minutes later. They will have been flying at low altitudes for longer, taking off in Iraq, crossing into Syria, and then across the border into Israel.

The "swarm" of drones and cruise missiles—as it will later be referred to—will have caught the country by surprise. By the time they strike, the target will be less relevant—the Haifa oil refinery, an apartment building in Kiryat Shmona, or a school in Katzrin.[11]

Katz continues:

This scenario, while fiction for now, is one that the IDF top brass is talking about on a regular basis these days. It is being played out in the minds of IDF generals and intelligence officials, responsible for watching Iran's every move, from Tehran all the way to its proxies' bases in Yemen, Iraq, Syria and the Gaza Strip.

The model is very similar to Iran's attack against the Aramco oil facility in Saudi Arabia in September: within the span of 17 minutes, 18 drones and three low-flying missiles hit the facility with amazing precision.[12]

CONCLUSION

The Iranian regime in Tehran is fixated on destroying the "Great Satan," America, and the "Little Satan," Israel. Ezekiel 38–39, written around 571 BC, prophesies an invasion of Israel by a coalition of Islamic nations, including Iran as a key player.

The war of Gog and Magog hasn't occurred yet, but the final showdown prophesied in Ezekiel is coming. How soon it will happen is outside our current ability to know. However, Israel's war with Iran and its proxies is a major piece to the puzzle that seems to be falling into place.

Keep watching the Middle East. But remember: Israel is on God's prophetic clock—and the hands are approaching midnight.

ISRAEL'S FUTURE IN SEVEN WORDS

- **Treaty**

  Under the direction of a Western leader, the Antichrist, who will guarantee peace and security, Israel will ink a treaty with him and possibly her neighbors (Daniel 9:27).

- **Temple**

  Israel will build the third temple in the end times (Matthew 24:15; 2 Thessalonians 2:4; Revelation 11:1–2).

- **Trap**

  The battle of Gog and Magog will be a surprise attack when Israel has let down her guard under the treaty with the West (Ezekiel 38–39).

- **Traitor**

  With the power vacuum created by the destruction of the Russian-Islamic axis, the Antichrist will break his treaty with Israel at the midpoint and consolidate his global rule (Daniel 9:27).

- **Trouble**

  Israel will endure the great Tribulation (Jeremiah 30:7).

- **Turning**

  As Christ returns to earth, many in Israel will turn to Him and receive Him as Messiah and Lord (Zechariah 12:10).

- **Triumph**

  Jesus will come to rescue the remnant of Israel and establish His one-thousand-year reign on the earth. During this era, the covenants God made with Israel will be literally and completely fulfilled (Revelation 20:1–6).

CHAPTER 8

WILL AMERICA SURVIVE?

America is in trouble. Big trouble. As a nation we are dancing on a perilous precipice, teetering on the verge of destruction. Aside from known threats of global terror, a Middle East meltdown, a soaring national debt, and the divisive spirit that has split our nation in two, our country's very foundations are cracking beneath our feet. America is losing her soul.
—JEFF KINLEY, *THE END OF AMERICA*

It is said that in the year 1787, a Scottish history professor named Alexander Fraser Tytler observed the following about the longevity of democracy:

A democracy is always temporary in nature; it simply cannot exist as a permanent form of government. A democracy will continue to exist up until the time that voters discover that they can vote themselves generous gifts from the public treasury. From that moment on, the majority always votes for the candidates who promise the most benefits from the public treasury, with the result that every democracy will finally collapse due to loose fiscal policy, which is always followed by a dictatorship.

The average age of the world's greatest civilizations from the beginning of history, has been about two hundred years. During those two hundred years, these nations always progressed through the following sequence:

From bondage to spiritual faith;
From spiritual faith to great courage;
From courage to liberty;
From liberty to abundance;
From abundance to complacency;
From complacency to apathy;
From apathy to dependence;
From dependence back into bondage.[1]

Based on any realistic evaluation, America is sliding toward the bottom of Professor Tytler's list. Abundance, apathy, and complacency abound. Dependence and bondage could be waiting in the wings.

The United States, while still prospering financially and wielding great military might, seems to be in trouble on numerous fronts. The status of the world's greatest superpower is not as firm as it has been in the past. Current events are magnifying cracks in the foundation. From the prophetic perspective, this raises important questions—questions about what role, if any, America plays in the end-time picture set forth in the Bible. When considering the showdown with Iran, and all its prophetic implications for Israel, the world, and the Middle East, it's fitting to briefly assess America's future. The place of America in Bible prophecy is probably the most asked question about the end times.

AMERICAN ABSENCE

An impressive list of modern nations (or their ancient counterpart) are referenced in end-time prophecies found in Scripture.

Israel	Central Asia (Magog)
Jordan (Ammon, Moab, and Edom)	Syria
	Greece
Egypt	Saudi Arabia and other
Sudan (Cush)	Gulf States (Sheba
Russia (Rosh)	and Dedan)
Iran (Persia)	Libya (Put)
Iraq (Babylon)	Lebanon (Tyre)
Europe (reunited Roman Empire)	

Some would add China or other far eastern nations to this list. They find them in the reference to the "kings from the east" in Revelation 16:12.

Noticeably absent from this list is America. All agree that

America is never explicitly mentioned in the pages of Scripture. The Bible never uses the word "America," nor does it say, "the United States." However, through the years, prophecy teachers have isolated several Scriptures they believe could be symbolic references to America. Some of the more notable ones are:

- Isaiah 18: the unnamed nation
- Ezekiel 38:13: the "young lions" or "merchants of Tarshish"
- Revelation 17–18: Babylon the Great

There's another view that holds America is the ten lost tribes of Israel.

Having examined each of these views in detail, I don't believe any of them directly refer to America.[2] I don't believe America is mentioned *directly* or *indirectly* in Scripture. Joel Rosenberg agrees:

> The truth is, the United States of America simply is nowhere to be found in the Bible. This may be painful for many to hear. This may be difficult for many to accept. Nevertheless, the fact remains: The US is never directly mentioned or specifically referenced in Bible history or in Bible prophecy. It just isn't.[3]

America's absence from the end-time picture raises the "why" question. Why is America missing in action in end-time prophecy? One obvious possibility is that America is simply not mentioned, just like most other nations. End-time prophecy shines the spotlight primarily on Israel and the Middle East, so America may just be omitted for that reason. While that's certainly possible, end-time prophecies do include Russia, Turkey, and the kings of the East, all of which lie outside the Middle East, so including America would not necessarily be a stretch. So what are we to make, if anything, of the scriptural silence concerning America in the end times?

While there is certainly room for disagreement on this point, I believe the lack of any mention of America in the end times is a clue that something must happen to America to lower her from superpower status before the end times begin. After all, it would be strange to omit any reference to the world's greatest superpower in end-time events if America is still the greatest nation on earth. Assuming it's true that America's absence from end-time prophecy is an indication that America is no longer the world's dominant power, what will happen to significantly decrease America's influence? What are some plausible scenarios to explain American absence from end-time prophecy?

Let me briefly suggest five possibilities.

1. ECONOMIC IMPLOSION

While considering possible reasons for the future fall of the United States, the list must include the growing debt bomb. The US total debt and annual budget deficit continue to balloon with no end in sight. The numbers have grown so large that it's difficult to wrap our minds around. America is now $23 trillion in debt and counting . . . and counting. The US treasury racks up an additional trillion every 365 days. You read that right. In just one year (2019) the annual budget deficit hit $1 trillion. America racked up another $1 trillion in debt, with no slowdown anywhere in sight. America is awash in debt, and even more troubling is that no one seems that worried about it. Politicians go on as if a day of reckoning will never come.

One problem we all face is that the human mind has trouble understanding a figure so massive. Here are some shocking facts that help put into perspective just how large $23 trillion really is.

- To pay down our national debt you would have to combine the GDP of China, Japan, and India.
- The United States owes $68,400 *per citizen*.
- The United States owes $183,000 *per taxpayer*.
- The United States currently has $125 trillion in unfunded liabilities.
- For the fiscal year 2019, interest alone on the federal debt is $479 billion.
- By 2025, the cost of servicing our national debt will exceed the cost of our military spending.
- It would take the United States 713,470 years to pay down the national debt if we paid $1 per second of the year.
- Modern presidents have doubled the national debt every nine years.[4]

To balance this gloomy debt picture, it's important to note that the US economy has enjoyed a great run over the past few years. The fiscal policies of President Trump have created increased wealth and prosperity in every stratum of society. Unemployment is down, earnings are up, and the stock market has performed well. The bulls are running. But how much longer can the reckless spending spree go on? When will the debt anchor exert such a downward pull that meaningful recovery is no longer feasible? When will America run out of money to fund her military and defend herself?

Runaway debt, ending in economic implosion, could spell American decline.

2. NUCLEAR NIGHTMARE

Another circumstance that could bring about America's demise is a nuclear 9/11. As nuclear proliferation spirals out of control, rogue nations such as Pakistan, North Korea, or Iran—if and when they get the bomb—could transfer a nuclear device or even a dirty bomb to a terrorist cell to detonate on American soil. Nuclear terror could trigger all kinds of consequences, bringing America to its knees.

3. MORAL CAVE-IN

God is merciful and patient. We should all be thankful for His goodness and grace to sinners, demonstrated in the sacrifice of Jesus. Nevertheless, the Bible is clear that God's wrath is not stored up forever. The righteous, holy God is justly angry against human sin. His judgment falls on nations as well as individuals.

The wrath of God is not a very popular topic. It never has been. However, the Bible presents at least four aspects of God's wrath.

1. **Direct wrath** is a cataclysmic outpouring of God's judgment. Some examples of this are the global flood (Genesis 7–8), the destruction of Sodom and Gomorrah (Genesis 19), and the plagues of Egypt (Exodus 7–11).

2. **Eschatological or end-time wrath** (also known as "Day of the Lord wrath") is the judgment of God poured out on earth during the future time of global Tribulation described in Revelation 6–19. The New Testament teaches that the church of Jesus Christ will be exempted from this time of wrath (1 Thessalonians 1:9–10; 5:9; Revelation 3:10–11). Jesus will come to rescue His bride before it begins.

3. **Eternal wrath** is the final form of God's wrath in the lake of fire, where the lost will experience separation from God (Revelation 14:9–11; 20:10, 15).

4. **Abandonment wrath** is a lesser-known form of God's wrath. It occurs when God actively pushes a person or nation in the direction they've already chosen and then removes His hand, "letting go" of that person or nation without any blessing or intervention to help them.

So far, by God's grace, America has not experienced the direct wrath of God, but could the United States be suffering abandonment wrath that will lead to an outpouring of God's direct wrath? Are there signs it has begun? How can we know? What does that look like?

Romans 1:21–32 is the clearest passage in the New Testament on God's "letting go" of a person or nation. Notice the threefold repetition of the words "God gave them over" (Romans 1:24, 26, 28). This is the wrath of abandonment—God removing His hand and His help. These verses reveal that abandonment wrath unfolds little by little. It's a deadly, downward spiral. "Abandonment is a gradual release that occurs in stages. And yet, like birth pangs, it seems to intensify toward a dramatic climax of corruption."[5] Four stages or phases can be traced in Romans 1:21–32.

- Stage 1: Rejection of God

  "For even though they knew God, they did not honor Him as God or give thanks, but they became futile in their speculations, and their foolish heart was darkened. Professing to be wise, they became fools, and exchanged the glory of the incorruptible God for an image in the form of corruptible man and of birds and four-footed animals and crawling creatures." (Romans 1:21–23)

- Stage 2: Rampant Sexual Immorality

  "Therefore God gave them over in the lusts of their hearts to impurity, so that their bodies would be dishonored among them. For they exchanged the truth of God for a lie, and worshiped and served the creature rather than the Creator, who is blessed forever. Amen." (Romans 1:24–25)

- Stage 3: Revolution of Homosexuality

  "For this reason God gave them over to degrading passions; for their women exchanged the natural function for that which is unnatural, and in the same way also the men abandoned the natural function of the woman and burned in their desire toward one another, men with men committing indecent acts and receiving in their own persons the due penalty of their error." (Roman 1:26–27)

- Stage 4: Ratification of Evil

  "And just as they did not see fit to acknowledge God any longer, God gave them over to a depraved mind, to do those things which are not proper, being filled with all unrighteousness, wickedness, greed, evil; full of envy, murder, strife, deceit, malice; they are gossips, slanderers, haters of God, insolent, arrogant, boastful, inventors of evil, disobedient to parents, without understanding, untrustworthy, unloving, unmerciful; and although they know the ordinance of God, that those who practice such things are worthy of death, they not only do the same, but also give hearty approval to those who practice them." (Romans 1:28–32)

The presence and progression of these stages does not indicate that God will judge a nation but that He already is judging. According to Romans 1, America is already under the judgment of God.

Rejection of God is the first domino that triggers the moral meltdown. That's stage 1 in the abandonment cycle—rejecting God. Tragically, when people lose God, they lose themselves, and moral confusion and chaos ensue. By any metric, we've witnessed a seismic moral shift in America in the past two decades. Moral thresholds are being crossed with alarming speed. Just when you think it can't get any worse, another descending step is uncovered. We live in a *Fifty Shades of Grey* culture. Pornography is pervasive. Here are just a few sobering statistics.

- There are 25 million pornographic websites.
- 40 million people regularly visit these sites.
- Almost eight in ten Americans visit a pornographic website at least once a month.[6]

American society is soaked in sexual sin. That's stage 2.

The atrocity of abortion stalks our land. Thankfully, abortion rates in America are steadily declining, but the tragic news is that the number is still close to one million per year!

One of the signs that a nation is being abandoned by God is the acceptance and sanctioning of homosexuality. Today in America, same-sex marriage is settled law. Any opposition to same-sex marriage or even questioning of it brings the wrath of the culture and the media. Gender confusion is growing. Transgenderism and "gender fluidity" are proliferating. Gender options today range anywhere from two to eighty-two. That's stage 3.

As Main Thing Ministries founder Jeff Kinley noted, "Spiritual decadence is a black hole, and its gravitational pull is sucking our nation into inescapable darkness."[7] Immorality of every kind is not just tolerated, it's protected and celebrated. That's stage 4.

America appears to be on the road to divine abandonment. This could be another leading factor in America's final fall.

4. CIVIL WAR II

One frightening possibility that could explain America's absence from end-time prophecy and apparent demise is a civil war—a total fracturing and dissolution of the nation. This would have been unthinkable even a few years ago, but the chasm between left and right is widening to what increasingly looks like a point of no return. Rabid partisanship and poisonous politics are rampant on every conceivable issue. The middle of the road seems to be the road less traveled more than ever before.

In light of the rising polarization in our public discourse in recent years, talk of a second US civil war has increased. When I first heard about this, I thought it was nothing more than further reckless rhetoric by conspiracy theorists and fanatics, which I try to avoid. However, a growing number of respected experts are noting that the political environment in the United States is the most divided it's been since the Civil War. Political analyst Bill Schneider, a professor of policy, government, and international affairs at George Mason University, opines, "Nothing is ever permanent, but we are broken. I'd say this is the most divided we've been since the Civil War."[8]

There's no doubt the United States is currently locked in a fierce ideological, political, and cultural civil war. Few would dispute that. Some refer to the current state of affairs as a "soft" civil war that's already underway in America, observed in the tearing of the racial, political, social, and ideological fabric. But could the ideological, political civil war spiral out of control, overflow the banks, and descend into a violent war? More and more people seem to think so.

Steve Chapman, a member of the *Chicago Tribune*'s editorial board, observed:

> Modern America is sharply polarized, battered by political furies and divided as never before. Moderation is disappearing, we are told, as Americans increasingly shun people of different views. We are split between hostile groups, each with its own TV networks, fast-food chains and sporting apparel—Fox News vs. MSNBC, Chick-fil-A vs. Chipotle, Under Armour vs. Nike. . . . Extreme, vocal ideologues are gaining ground on both the right and the left. One-third of likely voters, a poll found, think we are on the verge of civil war.[9]

Speaking after the House voted along party lines to approve a measure establishing procedures for the impeachment inquiry, Representative Louie Gohmert, a Republican from Texas, said that House Democrats were "about to push this country to a civil war if they were to get their wishes." He then added, "And if there's one thing I don't want to see in my lifetime, I don't want to ever have participation in, it's a civil war. Some historian, I don't remember who, said, guns are only involved in the last phase of a civil war."[10]

Civil war is a scary scenario to even think about, but more and more the ingredients seem to be simmering. Polarization abounds on every front. The nation is divided into two hostile camps on almost every issue. Common ground and compromise are increasingly elusive. President Trump has become a lightning rod for the Left. Commentator and political analyst Bill O'Reilly noted:

> As a person who loves America and many of the people in it, the specter of a civil war over Donald Trump is depressing. But that's exactly what's happening. . . . As things continue to devolve, anger is growing on both sides but more in the pro-Trump precincts. I fear violence might be next.[11]

Many triggers for a second civil war are possible. The following list is a rundown of some of the more conspicuous recent flashpoints.

- anarchist groups such as *antifa*
- racial tensions
- white supremacists
- angry clashes over the meaning and extent of the Second Amendment
- the Mueller Report
- constant partisan committee hearings in Congress
- immigration
- global warming

- capitalism versus socialism
- talk of certain states seceding from the Union
- Senate hearings for the Supreme Court nomination of Brett Kavanaugh
- impeachment hearings for President Trump
- Donald Trump, the President of the United States, being unwelcome and even actively excluded from many cities in America
- celebrities being blacklisted for showing friendliness to the president

A *Washington Post* headline reads, "In America, talk turns to something not spoken of for 150 years: Civil war." The story references, among others, Stanford University historian Victor Davis Hanson, who asked in a *National Review* essay last summer, "How, when, and why has the United States now arrived at the brink of a veritable civil war?" Dr. Hanson warns, "Almost every cultural and social institution—universities, the public schools, the NFL, the Oscars, the Tonys, the Grammys, late-night television, public restaurants, coffee shops, movies, TV, stand-up comedy—has been not just politicized but also weaponized. [The US stands] at the brink of a veritable civil war."[12]

Another *Washington Post* story reported Iowa Republican Congressman Steve King's posting a meme warning that red states have "8 trillion bullets" in the event of a civil war. And a poll conducted last June by Rasmussen Reports found that 31 percent of probable US voters surveyed believe "it's likely that the United States will experience a second civil war sometime in the next five years."[13] Almost half of black Americans believe another civil war is imminent.[14]

The idea of civil war may not be as far-fetched as some believe. "The sabre-rattling is getting louder. Governors. Judges. Preachers. Politicians. All are ramping-up the rhetoric, pushing the deep political divide within the United States towards a second Civil War."[15]

We pray this will never happen, but it could, and it would plunge the United States into oblivion.

5. THE GREAT DISAPPEARANCE

While any of these scenarios are possible alone or in a deadly combination, taking all the facts into account, my view is that the final fall of America will occur as a result of the rapture of all believers to heaven. The Bible predicts that a day is coming when the bride of Jesus Christ will be suddenly whisked away to heaven in the time it takes to blink. All over the earth, believers will suddenly disappear.

The rapture is not an event that was made up by wishful believers. Belief in the rapture is based on the clear teaching of Scripture. In John 14:1–3, Jesus promised to come back for His followers to take them to heaven.

"Do not let your heart be troubled; believe in God, believe also in Me. In My Father's house are many dwelling places; if it were not so, I would have told you; for I go to prepare a place for you. If I go and prepare a place for you, I will come again and receive you to Myself, that where I am, there you may be also."

The apostle Paul spoke often of the coming of Christ to remove or rapture His people from earth to heaven.

"Behold, I tell you a mystery; we will not all sleep, but we will all be changed, in a moment, in the twinkling of an eye, at the last trumpet; for the trumpet will sound, and the dead will be raised imperishable, and we will be changed. For the perishable must put on the imperishable, and this mortal must put on immortality" (1 Corinthians 15:51–53).

Writing to the Thessalonians, Paul highlighted the resurrection of deceased believers and the rapture of those who are alive when Jesus comes.

For this we say to you by the word of the Lord, that we who are alive and remain until the coming of the Lord, will not precede those who have fallen asleep. For the Lord Himself will descend from heaven with a shout, with the voice of the archangel and with the trumpet of God, and the dead in Christ will rise first. Then we who are alive and remain will be caught up together with them in the clouds to meet the Lord in the air, and so we shall always be with the Lord. Therefore comfort one another with these words. (1 Thessalonians 4:15–18)

The words "caught up" in 1 Thessalonians 4:17 translate the Greek word *harpazo*, which refers to the catching away of the church to heaven. When the Bible was translated from Greek to Latin by Jerome, he translated the word *harpazo* with the Latin word *rapio*, from which we get our English word *rapture*. The concept of a future rapture, or catching away of believers to heaven, is based on sound scriptural interpretation.

When the rapture occurs, every believer in America and all over the earth will be immediately transported to heaven, leaving those who are left behind to pick up the pieces of a shriveled workforce and shattered economy, not to mention the psychological trauma and fear that will prevail. While there are believers in every nation, about 5 to 10 percent of Americans profess faith in Jesus Christ alone for salvation from sin. The sudden removal of twenty to thirty million people from the United States would be apocalyptic (literally).

Prophecy teacher Jeff Kinley painted a graphic picture of America in the aftermath of the rapture:

> So imagine what will happen when both the salt and the light is removed from today's culture. Who will be left behind to preserve decency, morality, and goodness? Who will expose and penetrate the darkness? . . . Not a single believer on American soil. Imagine that for a moment. . . . With our country's soul now removed, she will become a zombie-like nation, wandering aimlessly toward her ultimate and inevitable demise. . . . In this miraculous moment,

the complete departure of Christians is not the only thing that will change. Everything will be altered following that split-second departure—governments, states, communities, militaries, schools, churches, colleges, hospitals, universities, families, marriages, national infrastructures . . . *everything*. There won't be a single pocket of society that remains unaffected, as for all practical purposes, God will have "left the building."[16]

Kinley concluded his somber description of post-rapture America:

What follows is political, economic, and moral chaos in this country. . . . A colossal void of truth will be left behind. And unrestrained sin will begin swallowing up an entire society. All across the country, the scenario will become one of confusion, chaos, and fear, resulting in rampant crime, robberies, and murders. A nationwide panic attack will grip the country. . . . Because of the rapture, a significant portion of America's population will be gone, leaving huge voids in virtually every strata [*sic*] of society. . . . With anarchy and chaos reigning, America will be paralyzed, and officially no longer a major player in world affairs.

Like a heavy blanket, darkness falls on an entire nation. . . . In the time it takes you to bat an eye, our country will be transformed from the Land of the Free to the Home of the Abandoned. Before the sun rises, she will go from being a global superpower to a drowning nation struggling to survive. . . . . It's Jesus' rescue of His bride from a rebellious planet that will pull the pin, ignite public pandemonium, and usher in an unprecedented moment in human history.[17]

Of course, the rapture could occur in concert with some of the other scenarios outlined above, plunging the late great United States into a national free fall.

KEEP GOING

While no one on earth knows for sure what will happen to the United States in the end times, the lack of any biblical mention of America as a key player does not bode well for continued American greatness and dominance.

Knowing this should not cause us to give up and do nothing—to throw up our hands in despair. We need to continue to do three main things. First, fervently pray for our nation and its leaders every day (1 Timothy 2:1–2).

Second, we must strive to live godly, righteous lives as salt and light in an increasingly decaying and darkening world. Proverbs 14:34 reminds us that "righteousness exalts a nation."

Third, America needs to maintain support for Israel, so she can experience the promise to those who bless Israel (Genesis 12:1–3). President Trump has honored the Jewish people by recognizing the Golan Heights as part of Israeli territory and declaring that Israeli settlements in the West Bank do not violate international law. In spite of the United States' shortcomings, I believe God's hand of blessing remains upon this land, at least to some degree, for our support of Israel.

We do all these things as we await the coming of Jesus. No one knows when He will come. We need to be ready all the time and do what we can while we can in His service.

CHAPTER 9

HOPE FOR TODAY

*I keep a Bible open on my desk to remind me
of God and His Word, and The Truth.*
—US Secretary of State Mike Pompeo, in a
speech at the American University in Cairo

It is a never-ending struggle . . . until the rapture.
—US Secretary of State Mike Pompeo, on current
events, Summit Church, Wichita, Kansas, in
2015, while serving as a US congressman

When I was growing up, I had a friend down the street whose mother loved puzzles. Really big, complicated puzzles with very small pieces. I was never patient enough to put together any puzzle that took longer than an hour, so I was amazed by these puzzles that would fill an entire table in their game room for months at a time as she carefully plugged each piece in place. Watching the process, I learned that a puzzle master must consult the picture on the top of the box as the template for the final product. You have to have the final picture in view. I also learned that the best way to construct a puzzle is to begin with the corner and edge pieces to establish a frame and then to work toward the middle.

The same is true of the end-time prophetic puzzle. The end-time picture set forth in Scripture is the picture on top of the box. When all the pieces are finally in place, that's what it will look like. As we look at our world today, events are beginning to closely match the picture on the puzzle box. All the puzzle pieces aren't in place, but the corners and edges have taken form. The framework is set. The center of the puzzle is ready to be filled in.

Israel is back in her ancient homeland after almost two thousand years of dispersion. Russia is rising. Iran is increasing. Russia and Iran are allied for the first time in history. Turkey is turning to Russia and Iran. Russia and Iran are positioned in Syria on Israel's northern doorstep. The alliance of Ezekiel 38 is developing and deepening. Anti-Semitism is surging. Iran and the United States keep moving toward the brink of war, only to back away at the last moment. The Middle East, the biblical staging ground for the end times, is the focus of the world's attention.

As the prophetic puzzle takes shape, the world seems to be teetering on the brink of chaos, especially in the Middle East. Tensions are running high. Nerves are on edge. People everywhere are hoping for the best, a peaceful resolution of the conflict, but fearing the worst. We want some reassurance. We want to know where it's all headed and how it will end.

This raises a critical question: How should we live in light of what's unfolding in our world? In light of what lies ahead? What should we do? How can we find peace in the storm and make sure we're ready when Jesus comes? Many people have the mistaken idea that Bible prophecy isn't relevant to everyday life. That it has no practical application. I disagree. Bible prophecy is supremely relevant and practical. God gave prophecy to change our hearts, not to cram our heads with knowledge. Eschatology leads to ethics. Believing Jesus can come at any moment must change what we do and what we don't do.

While there are many practical implications of knowing what's coming, let me suggest five simple, practical points of application for you to make part of your thinking and living that will make a difference in your life today.

1. RECOGNIZE THE BIBLE IS TRUE

Humans can't resist the temptation to try to forecast the future. This inclination increases in troubled times. One of the go-to sources people appeal to is the sixteenth-century French prognosticator and alleged seer Nostradamus. People believe Nostradamus has accurately predicted all kinds of things. One Nostradamus text allegedly forewarns of a global conflict unfolding in 2020. The Nostradamus prophecy reads, "Twice put up and twice cast down, the East will also weaken the West." Another reads, "Its adversary after several battles chased by sea will fail at time of need." Some point to another Nostradamus quatrain as relating to President Trump, which includes "The great man will be struck down in the day by a thunderbolt. An evil deed, foretold by the bearer of a petition."[1]

Of course, these vague statements have nothing to do with the year 2020 or global conflict, but that doesn't stop people from trying to grasp at anything, no matter how unreliable, to peer into the future.

As 2019 drew to a close, *USA Today* included an article on predictions people had made years earlier about what would happen by 2020. Here are a few of them:

- Mathematician and scientist D. G. Brennan predicted that by 2018 people would have jetpacks.
- Brennan wrote in 1968, "I shall not be surprised if on my 92nd birthday I am able to go for a ride in an anti-gravity car."
- Futurist Ray Kurzweil predicted in 1999 that human life expectancy would rise to "over one hundred" by 2019.
- Kurzweil had several other prophecies for the year 2019, including invisible computers.
- In 1968, physicist Herman Kahn and futurist Anthony J. Weiner said that by 2020 Americans would work 1,370 hours a year (or 26 hours a week), instead of the 1,940 hours (37 hours a week) that was average at the time.
- In 1968, Ithiel de Sola Pool, a political science professor at the Massachusetts Institute of Technology, predicted

that better communication, easier translation, and greater understanding of the nature of human motivations would make it easier for people to connect across ethnic and national lines. "By the year 2018 nationalism should be a waning force in the world," he wrote.[2]

These are just a few of the better-known predictions, but I'm sure many people had personal predictions about what life would be like in 2020. While a few of them may have come true, man's résumé of accurately predicting the future is very thin. We don't even know what will happen tomorrow. But the Bible does. There's an old saying, "If you want to know what happened yesterday, read the newspaper; if you want to know what happened today, listen to the evening news; if you want to know what will happen tomorrow, read the Bible." As we've seen, the Bible is a book of prophecy. Hundreds of prophecies have been fulfilled, many related to ancient Persia—modern-day Iran.

While the rise of militant Islam has shocked and surprised most people, amazingly, more than twenty-five hundred years ago, God, through the prophet Ezekiel, predicted the exact scenario that we see developing before our eyes every day on the evening news. Ezekiel 36–39 is "history written beforehand." It foretells the regathering of the Jewish people to their ancient homeland, the animosity the surrounding nations will have for Israel, and the invasion of Israel by those nations.

God predicted all these things with piercing precision.

Seven times in Ezekiel 38–39 we read the same words, "Thus says the Lord God" (38:3, 10, 14, 17; 39:1, 17, 25). Another eight times we see the refrain, "declares the Lord GOD." Obviously, God doesn't want us to miss the point—this is His Word. The prediction in Ezekiel 38–39 comes directly from Him. He is the author of the script. The Bible is true. Fulfilled prophecy proves it.

We can rest assured that the biblical predictions that are still unfulfilled will come to pass. We can also rest assured that what the Bible tells us about God, Jesus, salvation, sin, and our own lives is trustworthy and reliable.

So, recognize the Bible is true and to read it regularly. Soak in its truth and apply its instruction to your daily life. It will transform you.

2. REALIZE YOUR NEED FOR JESUS

The Bible not only accurately predicts the future, it also accurately portrays the human condition apart from God. The inspired, inerrant Word of God truthfully, transparently diagnoses the condition of every person. It tells that we have all sinned and are falling short of God's righteous standard (Romans 3:23). That's the bad news—the *really* bad news. Every person on earth is sinful and separated from God. We constantly miss the mark of perfection. We're born that way. And there's nothing on our own we can do about our predicament. No amount of church attendance, good works, helping the poor, or praying can ever forgive our sins.

You and I can't get rid of one of our sins on our own, let alone the thousands of transgressions that pile up throughout our lives. The Bible is clear that our sins can only be washed away by the blood of Jesus Christ, that is, His death for us. His death in our place.

Jesus is the only Mediator, the only go-between who can bridge the chasm between a holy God and sinful people. He is your only hope for heaven. No one will be in heaven without personally trusting in Him for salvation.

If you've never received Jesus as your Savior from sin, that's the first thing you need to do before you do anything else. He is life. He is truth. He is the way to God. Here are three simple steps to guide you to trusting in Jesus.

First, admit you're a sinner. That shouldn't be too difficult to do. We all know the guilt we feel when we do things that hurt others or ourselves. You and I know we're sinful and fallen.

Second, acknowledge that you can't do anything to save yourself—that you need a Savior.

Third, accept Jesus Christ as your Savior. He's the Savior you need. Receive the payment He offered on the cross for your sins. The Bible says we become children of God, part of His family, by receiving Jesus as our Savior and Lord (John 1:12–13).

Why not receive Him now? Why not receive the pardon He purchased for you when He died on the cross and rose again on the third day?

3. REMEMBER GOD IS IN CONTROL

More and more today our world seems out of control. We live in a world of cascading crises. Violence is mushrooming. Volcanoes are spewing ash all over the planet. Natural disasters are becoming more commonplace and destructive. The earth itself is groaning. Seemingly unsolvable problems plague our nation and global community.

Dr. David Jeremiah said it well: "I can understand why people shudder at today's headlines. The daily news shows an alarming disintegration of world order and security. We see growing disorder now and chaos ahead, and we wonder whether God has turned His face away from us."[3]

Then he told this humorous story:

Some years ago, the late pastor Ray Stedman was scheduled to speak at a conference in England. Each session of the conference began with a song service. One night, the leader led the worshippers in the chorus "Our God Reigns." Stedman glanced at the song sheet, which had been prepared by the church staff. What he saw caused him to smile. Someone, intending to type the title as "Our God Reigns," had actually typed "Our God Resigns."

Jeremiah concluded:

Let me assure you that our God will never resign. We who trust Him have no reason to fear. As I have read Ezekiel 38–39, the one thing that stands out is the sovereignty of God. He is in control. God orchestrates this scenario to demonstrate to His people, Israel, that He is their God and worthy of their trust. Israel has no hope without God, and God will win the battle for the nation. Godless Russia is no match for the King of kings.

The God of Israel is also our God, which means whatever we fear is also no match for the King of kings. When it looks like there is no hope, hope is just waiting for the proper moment to show up. God can be trusted.[4]

Ezekiel 38–39 reveals that God is in control. Over and over in these chapters, God makes it clear that He is in charge. If there's one thing we learn from this passage above all else, it's that God is on top of things. God's control is evident to such an extent that the prophet encourages the readers by telling them the end of the story before it even begins.[5] He wrote the script; He assembled the cast; He's making sure the stage is perfectly set for His great prophetic production. He's the Director of the entire drama.

That's not only true of nations and leaders; it's true in all of life. In your life. In my life. God knows the end of the story before it begins. He knew the end of your story and of my story before our lives began. The same God who has the whole world in His hands has your world in His hands. God is in control of your life. And His Son, Jesus, is Lord. He can provide for you and protect you in the daily troubles and turbulence of life.

I like the story of a New Zealand pilot named Owen B. Wilson, who wanted to do something special for his friend's birthday. Wilson offered to take his friend flying in his small two-seat aircraft. They departed on a Sunday afternoon after church and took in the splendor of the landscapes and seascapes that unfolded in a panorama before them. At one point, they crossed a tall mountain, and the engine began to sputter and then died. As the plane began quickly losing altitude, Wilson searched the area below to land but saw nothing but steep mountainside. When it appeared they would fly into a mountain, Wilson's passenger cried out, "Lord, please help us get over that steep ledge!"

They barely skimmed over the ridge and then began to pray for the Lord to show them somewhere to safely land. At the last moment, when all hope seemed lost, they spotted a tiny strip of land almost hidden between two ridges. They glided into the narrow opening, touched down, and bounced to a stop. In unison the men shouted, "Thank You, Lord!"

Looking up, just in front of them, they saw a big twenty-foot sign that said, "Jesus is Lord!"

As it turned out, a Christian retreat center owned the field, which explained the billboard. The owners ran out to meet their unexpected visitors and told them the field was normally filled with livestock, but on this day, the animals were lined along the edge of the field, as if giving them space to land.

Our world today is experiencing some major instability. The same can be true in our personal lives. We often find ourselves flying into turbulence. Sometimes the engines stall. Things might be so bad we find ourselves bracing for a crash. Circumstances seem hopeless. But whatever the situation we can discover the incredible truth that Jesus is Lord.[6] Our God is in control and in charge.

4. REMAIN HOPEFUL

There are many competing philosophies in the world, but when it all boils down, there are really just two: hope and despair. Without Jesus Christ and His Word, all other philosophies ultimately end in existential gloom.

Max Lucado observed:

> We live in a day of despair. The suicide rate in American has increased 24 percent since 1999. Twenty-four percent! If a disease saw such a spike, we would deem it an epidemic. How do we explain the increase? We've never been more educated. We have tools of technology our parents could not have dreamed of. We are saturated with entertainment and recreation. Yet more people than ever are orchestrating their own deaths. How would this be?
>
> Among the answers must be this: people are dying for lack of hope. Secularism sucks the hope out of society. It reduces the world to a few decades between birth and hearse. Many people believe this world is as good as it gets, and let's face it. It's not that good.
>
> But people of the promise have an advantage. . . . They filter life through the promises of God.[7]

That's a great description of those who know Jesus Christ—"people of the promise." God has given His people many precious promises to strengthen us against discouragement and despair. According to one count, there are 7,487 promises in the Bible.

The Bible is a book of prophecy, but it's also a book of promises, and often the two are closely related.

One of the greatest prophecies of Scripture that's also a promise comes from Jesus. Nothing is more encouraging and energizing than the promise that Jesus is coming back to take His people to heaven to be with Him.

> Don't let your hearts be troubled. Trust in God, and trust also in me. There is more than enough room in my Father's home. If this were not so, would I have told you that I am going to prepare a place for you? When everything is ready, I will come and get you, so that you will always be with me where I am. (John 14:1–3 NLT)

It's been well said that hope is "oxygen for the soul." That's true. The ultimate hope for this world is the "blessed hope" of the coming of Jesus. He will come to catch away His people to heaven to rescue us from the coming time of tribulation on the earth. Then, after the Great Tribulation has run its course, we will return with Jesus to earth, and He will establish His rule and reign over the earth. The earth will be restored to God's original intentions. The world will never find peace through diplomacy and negotiation. Peace will only be achieved when the Prince of Peace splits the sky to return to earth.

The exciting thing about the promise of Jesus' coming is that He can return at any moment. He may not come for ten years, but He could come today. As followers of Jesus, we can get up every morning and say "perhaps today." Perhaps today may be the day Jesus comes.

This is our hope. In the end, it's our only hope. I once heard someone say, "Life with Christ is an endless hope, without him a hopeless end." Make sure you have Jesus and are looking forward to an endless hope when He comes.

5. REACH OUT TO OTHERS

When we're surrounded by trouble and filled with fear about the future, we can easily succumb to self-focus and living a self-absorbed life. All our time and energy can be exhausted on ourselves. Further, as we look at what's ahead, we can get too focused on the future and interpreting biblical prophecies that we lose our passion for reaching out to those who have never received the truth of the gospel. We can take our eye off the ball.

In his books and sermons, Vance Havner often cautioned believers not to get so caught up in the details of Bible prophecy that they fail to take their responsibility seriously to win people to Christ. In his book *It Is Time*, Havner wrote:

> I know that some are always studying the meaning of the fourth toe of the right foot of some beast in prophecy and have never used either foot to go and bring men to Christ. I do not know who the 666 is in Revelation but I know the world is

sick, sick, sick and the best way to speed the Lord's return is
to win more souls for Him.[8]

In all the things we do as we await the coming of Christ,
nothing is more important and urgent than spreading the message
of the gospel. Jesus can come at any moment, and the multiplying
signs indicate His coming could be very soon. Scripture even ties
our evangelistic efforts to the coming of Christ. We hasten His
coming by reaching the lost (2 Peter 3:9, 12).

By any measure, time is slipping away. We need a sense of
urgency to reach people who are lost and to fund the advance-
ment of the gospel in all places, including the chaotic Middle
East. We've talked a great deal in this book about the regime that
leads Iran, the menacing mullahcracy. They are evil and power-
hungry. However, we don't want to confuse the powers in Iran
with the people of Iran. We're called to love the people there who
are confined in a dark place. I don't want anything in this book
to be misinterpreted or misunderstood as malice toward Iranian
citizens. God loves the people of Iran. Jesus died for them. We
need to pray for them and do all we can to see the light of the
gospel pierce the darkness.

According to many sources, the gospel is expanding rapidly
in the Middle East, especially Iran. Many believe the church in
Iran is currently the fastest-growing segment of the church in
the world.[9] As the Iranian people see firsthand the emptiness of
Islam and the darkness of the mullah regime, they're turning in
droves to the light of the gospel. Iranian Muslims are fleeing to
Christ in record numbers. What's happening spiritually in Iran

is so significant and revolutionary it's been called "the Iranian Awakening."[10]

May the Lord help us continue to pray for the Iranian people, and all those in the Middle East, and for the Christian workers who are laboring there in difficult and dangerous circumstances to bring them the gospel of Jesus Christ. Time may be short.

LIVE LOOKING

Events are unfolding today in the Middle East and Israel with lightning speed. Unexpected twists and turns are the new norm. It can seem as if there's no rhyme or reason to it all. But according to God's Word, it's all part of the buildup to the end of days predicted in the Bible.

The signs of the times we're witnessing are like runway lights beginning to light up as the coming of Christ approaches.

Jesus can come at any moment.

Make sure you know Him. Make sure He's coming for you.

Seize the opportunities you have before they slip away.

Remain faithful in a world that's increasingly faithless and fearful. Remain faithful to Jesus, to His Word, and to His calling to reach the nations with the gracious gospel of life and peace. Live each day alert, aware, and active.

Jesus is coming.

ACKNOWLEDGMENTS

I thank God for the privilege to do what I love every day: study, teach, and write about His inspired, infallible Word. I'm mindful that few people get to do what they love every day, so I gratefully acknowledge God's kindness to me and never want to take it for granted. My acknowledgment of Him eclipses all else in importance.

At the center of all I do, other than the Lord, is my wife, Cheryl, who has made my life easy and enjoyable for more than three decades. She freely gives me herself and her time and with that I get her wisdom and insight, which I highly value. For our almost thirty-four years as marriage and ministry partners, God has been better to us than we would have ever dreamed. This book is another expression of God's grace to us, for which we give thanks.

As events continue to unfold in the Middle East, the folks at Nelson Books worked tirelessly to expedite the release of this book. That put a great deal of extra pressure on the editing team, but they've made it look easy and made me look much better than I am. I'm grateful they share my vision for helping people connect current events to biblical prophecy and then living in light of that truth. Their excellent work was spearheaded by senior editor Janene MacIvor. We have known of each other for years, but this is the first time I've had the privilege of partnering with Thomas Nelson and with her. Her kind spirit and excellent work in shepherding this book have inspired me. Renee Chavez and Lauren Langston Stewart are two other members of the core team of professionals who thoughtfully edited this book.

Of course, there's much more to a book than its writing and release. Thanks to all who've labored to promote, market, and increase the reach of this book. My daughter-in-law Natalee is the key to the team that keeps my social media in order and assists me with marketing. I appreciate her willingness and readiness to help her technologically challenged father-in-law. She never makes me feel dim or outdated.

I have the privilege of being represented by William K. Jensen, who is also a very close, dear friend. I value Bill's input, wisdom, and friendship greatly. God has blessed and honored our relationship over the years as we have sought to honor Him. Bill is always available as a listening ear and a valuable voice. I pray that God continues to give us the creativity and opportunity to continue to produce books that point people to Jesus and His coming.

The elders and members of Faith Bible Church, where I serve as Senior Pastor, have been and continue to be an anchor in my life. Their faithful support and constant encouragement energize me to fulfill God's calling on my life with joy. No pastor ever served a better church.

May the Lord use all our combined efforts, meager as they are, to bring abundant glory to His name and animate us to be ready when the trumpet sounds.

Dr. Mark Hitchcock
Edmond, Oklahoma,
February 2019

APPENDIX 1

THE ELAM PROPHECIES IN LIGHT OF CURRENT EVENTS IN IRAN

Many prophecy teachers believe that in addition to the reference to Iran in Ezekiel 38, modern Iran is mentioned in the Old Testament under the name "Elam." In a book about Iran in Bible prophecy, I thought it would be important and helpful to address this issue.

A primary proponent of the "Elam" view of modern Iran is Bill Salus. He outlines his position in his book *Nuclear Showdown in Iran: The Ancient Prophecy of Elam*. Salus contends that Jeremiah 49:34–39 and Ezekiel 32:24–25 are prophecies about the destruction of Iran in the end of days. He, and those who agree with him, are correct that ancient Elam was located in what today is Iran. The ancient nation of Elam was a warlike nation located two hundred miles east of Babylon.

Joel Rosenberg agrees with the future fulfillment of Jeremiah 49:34–39. He said, "We read the prophecy concerning the future judgment and blessed restoration of Elam (modern day Iran). . . . The judgment is described in verses 35 through 38. . . . Most importantly, we read in verse 38 that the Lord says that 'it will come about in the last days that I will restore the fortunes of Elam.' . . . This is critical because it gives us another indication that this is an End Times prophecy, consistent [with] the previous prophecies."[1]

The pertinent question is: Is everything in these prophecies about Elam in Jeremiah 49 and Ezekiel 32 still in the future for the nation of Iran, or have all or some parts of them already been fulfilled in ancient Elam? I don't have space here to interact with all the points on this issue, but I'll address it by briefly examining each of these prophecies in their context.

JEREMIAH 49

The first Old Testament prophecy of Elam is found in Jeremiah 49. This prophecy was given in 598–97 BC.

That which came as the word of the Lord to Jeremiah the prophet concerning Elam, at the beginning of the reign of Zedekiah king of Judah, saying:

"Thus says the LORD of hosts,

'Behold, I am going to break the bow of Elam,

The finest of their might.

'I will bring upon Elam the four winds

From the four ends of heaven,

And will scatter them to all these winds;

And there will be no nation

To which the outcasts of Elam will not go.

'So I will shatter Elam before their enemies

And before those who seek their lives;

And I will bring calamity upon them,

Even My fierce anger,' declares the LORD,

'And I will send out the sword after them

Until I have consumed them.

'Then I will set My throne in Elam

And destroy out of it king and princes,'

Declares the LORD.

'But it will come about in the last days

That I will restore the fortunes of Elam,'"

Declares the LORD. (Jeremiah 49:34–39)

Bill Salus maintains this is a separate end-time prophecy from Ezekiel 38–39 about the judgment of Iran. He sees two judgments of Iran in the end of days: "At this point, it's important to discuss Iran's double jeopardy in the latter days," he wrote. Iran is the subject of dual judgment prophecies, one in Jeremiah 49:34–39, and the other in Ezekiel 38 and 39. This means that the rogue nation will experience double trouble in the end times."[2] He focuses on the different settings for the two passages as the major clue that different judgments are in view; Jeremiah 49 as a conflict that occurs within Iran while the events in Ezekiel 38 take place in Israel.

Let me begin by saying that the reference to "the last days" in Jeremiah 49:39 clearly adds an end-time dimension to this prophecy when it speaks of God's restoration of Elam (or Iran) at the end of days. This plainly indicates a final restoration of Elam in the coming messianic kingdom. Jeremiah indicates that Elam's destruction will not be final or eternal. This should serve as an encouragement to every person. God's grace can cover the worst of sins. His dealings with Elam are a powerful picture of His grace and mercy toward sinners—grace that every person needs.

So while it's clear that the final part of this prophecy takes the reader to the end, the preceding context leads me to conclude that the bulk of this prophecy refers to a past destruction of Elam that was fulfilled long ago.

The reference in Jeremiah 49:35 to breaking "the bow of Elam" is appropriate because the ancient Elamites were famous for their archery skills. Ezekiel also prophesies that in her day of distress, invaders will attack Elam from every direction.

In the immediate setting, just before the prophecy of Elam's destruction, Jeremiah prophesied the destruction of two ancient nations—Kedar and Hazor (Jeremiah 49:28–33). He said they will be destroyed by Nebuchadnezzar, king of Babylon. This clearly refers to a past destruction of these nations by Nebuchadnezzar in the sixth century BC. The close connection of the prophecies about Kedar and Hazor that have already been fulfilled regarding the destruction of Elam indicates that it, too, has already happened. While not impossible, it would be strange in the immediate context for one prophecy to be fulfilled in the near future and the next one to speak completely about the end of days.

John Walvoord also sees a connection between the destruction of Kedar and Hazor by the Babylonians and the destruction of Elam. He said, "A brief prophecy concerning Kedar and Hazor is contained in Jeremiah 49:28–33. It is a prediction of judgment upon them at the hands of Nebuchadnezzar king of Babylon. A similar judgment is pronounced upon Elam in Jeremiah 49:34–38."[3]

Jeremiah 49:38 says that the Lord will set His throne in Elam "and destroy her king and officials." This somewhat cryptic phrase means that "the Lord Himself will sit in judgment of Elam."[4] It means that God will personally supervise Elam's devastation. The same imagery appears earlier in Jeremiah when describing Nebuchadnezzar's destruction of Egypt. "'Thus says the LORD of hosts, the God of Israel, "Behold, I am going to send and get Nebuchadnezzar the king of Babylon, My servant, and I am going to set his throne right over these stones that I have hidden; and he will spread his canopy over them"'" (Jeremiah 43:10). Bible teacher Warren Wiersbe observes: "Whenever a nation was defeated, the victors would set up their king's throne in the city gate (Jeremiah 1:15; 39:3; 43:8–13), and that's what God promised to do in Elam (49:38). He would let them know that He was King."[5]

Other than the final verse of Jeremiah 49, dealing with

Elam's final restoration, the context of Elam's destruction leads me to conclude this is referring to the historical destruction of Elam in the distant past, not a future judgment of the modern nation of Iran.

EZEKIEL 32

Ezekiel's prophecy of Elam in chapter 32 was recorded in 585 BC, about twelve years after Jeremiah's prediction. Bill Salus sees Ezekiel 32 as another end-time prophecy of Iran's destruction. He interpreted the reference in verse 24 to "terror in the land of the living" as a chilling reference to Iran's terrorist activities today. He said, "Ezekiel connects more prophetic dots by acknowledging that Elam is guilty of causing 'terror in the land of the living.' The prophet also mentions this fact two times in these verses. Iran is notably the world's foremost sponsor of international terror."[6]

However, in the immediate context, this same phrase is used of Assyria (32:23), Meshech and Tubal (32:24), and, in short form, the Sidonians (32:30). Elam is in no way singled out for its terrorizing actions. This doesn't refer to current Iranian terrorism, but to what these nations did in the ancient past.

As with Jeremiah 49, I believe the context indicates that Ezekiel's reference to Elam is a reference to a past, historical judgment of that nation, not an end-time prophecy. The mention of Elam in Ezekiel 32 is in a broader context related to the impending fall of Egypt. Ezekiel 32 is the prophet's sixth prophecy against Egypt. It is a sobering funeral dirge announcing Egypt's doom. The main point in Ezekiel 32 is that Egypt will be utterly destroyed and that her leader, Pharaoh, and her slain soldiers will descend into Sheol or the underworld.

To dramatize his point, Ezekiel employs a vivid image. He lists several other mighty nations who have fallen and whose armies will be waiting in the nether world when Pharaoh and his defeated army arrive. The waiting nations he mentions are: Assyria (modern Iraq), Elam (modern Iran), Meshech and Tubal (modern Turkey), Edom (modern Jordan), and Sidon (modern Lebanon).

In this setting, Ezekiel is unmistakably referring to defeated Elamites in his own day who were already in the grave, waiting for the arrival of the ancient Egyptians. Ezekiel's reference to Elamite soldiers who had already died precludes this prophecy from finding its fulfillment in the end of days. How could modern Iranian soldiers be waiting in the underworld for Egyptians who were destroyed more than two and a half millennia ago? That simply doesn't make any sense.

For these reasons I don't find any future prophecy of Iran in Jeremiah's or Ezekiel's references to Elam other than Jeremiah's beautiful prediction that Elam's fortunes will be restored in days to come.

IRAN'S PRESENCE IN SYRIA AND THE DESTRUCTION OF DAMASCUS IN ISAIAH 17

Syria is a key prophetic hot spot for both Islamic and Christian end-times enthusiasts.

According to Islamic teaching, two huge Islamic armies will square off in a great battle near Damascus in the end of days. Shia Muslims believe this war will precipitate the coming of the Mahdi, the Islamic messiah. This teaching played a major role in the focus of ISIS on Syria.

In a similar vein, many Christian students of end-time prophecy believe the Syrian capital, Damascus, plays a key end-time role. Based on Isaiah 17, they believe Damascus will be leveled in the end times, possibly by an Israeli nuclear strike. Many believe this event will transpire just before or just after the rapture of believers to heaven.

There's no disputing the fact that Syria has dominated world headlines in recent years.

The catastrophic civil war there has been raging since 2011, resulting in the death of more than five hundred thousand people and the displacing of almost seven million. ISIS placed a major focus on gaining land in Syria for its caliphate.

Iran has become a chief ally of Syria, bolstering the regime of Bashar al-Assad. It is deeply imbedded and entrenched in Syria. Iran is constructing a large-scale military base in Syria that will house thousands of troops.[1] The compound contains numerous large storehouses. Iran is in Syria for the long haul. Russia's substantial military presence in Syria has led some to refer to Vladimir Putin as the "King of Syria." At the same time and in concert with Russia, Turkey is seeking control of northern Syria.

With all this concentration and convergence in Syria, Israel is understandably concerned.

In response to the growing Iranian threat, Israeli fighters have pounded Iranian positions, resources, and weapons shipments in Syria in hundreds of strikes. Israel is determined not to allow Iran to get more entrenched without paying a heavy price. Iran is threatening that Israel "will regret" these attacks.[2]

The presence of Iran in Syria and Israel's strong military

response against that presence has led many to wonder if this could have a connection to Isaiah's prophecy of the destruction of Damascus (the capital of Syria) in Isaiah 17. Could the crisis ultimately reach such a point that Israel feels compelled to launch a devastating attack against Damascus, possibly even a nuclear option, to eliminate the Iranian threat.

Current events raise the issue of a connection between what's happening in Syria and the imminent fulfillment of the prophecy of the destruction of Damascus in Isaiah 17. In other words, does the Bible predict an end-time, complete destruction of Damascus?

The city of Damascus is mentioned fifty-six times in the New American Standard Bible.

Two important references to Damascus are found in prophetic sections of the Old Testament: Isaiah 17 and Jeremiah 49:23–27. We'll focus primarily on Isaiah 17:

The oracle concerning Damascus.

"Behold, Damascus is about to be removed from being a city
And will become a fallen ruin.
"The cities of Aroer are forsaken;
They will be for flocks to lie down in,
And there will be no one to frighten them.
"The fortified city will disappear from Ephraim,
And sovereignty from Damascus
And the remnant of Aram;
They will be like the glory of the sons of Israel,"
Declares the LORD of hosts.

Now in that day the glory of Jacob will fade,

And the fatness of his flesh will become lean.

It will be even like the reaper gathering the standing grain,

As his arm harvests the ears,

Or it will be like one gleaning ears of grain

In the valley of Rephaim.

Yet gleanings will be left in it like the shaking of an olive tree,

Two or three olives on the topmost bough,

Four or five on the branches of a fruitful tree,

Declares the LORD, the God of Israel.

In that day man will have regard for his Maker

And his eyes will look to the Holy One of Israel.

He will not have regard for the altars, the work of his hands,

Nor will he look to that which his fingers have made,

even the Asherim and incense stands.

In that day their strong cities will be like forsaken places in
     the forest,

Or like branches which they abandoned before the sons of
     Israel;

And the land will be a desolation.

For you have forgotten the God of your salvation

And have not remembered the rock of your refuge.

Therefore you plant delightful plants

And set them with vine slips of a strange god.

In the day that you plant it you carefully fence it in,

And in the morning you bring your seed to blossom;

But the harvest will be a heap

In a day of sickliness and incurable pain.

Alas, the uproar of many peoples
Who roar like the roaring of the seas,
And the rumbling of nations
Who rush on like the rumbling of mighty waters!
The nations rumble on like the rumbling of many waters,
But He will rebuke them and they will flee far away,
And be chased like chaff in the mountains before the wind,
Or like whirling dust before a gale.
At evening time, behold, there is terror!
Before morning they are no more.
Such will be the portion of those who plunder us
And the lot of those who pillage us.

As Joel Rosenberg notes,

"According to all major translations, the meaning
of the text is clear:

1. The passage concerns the city of Damascus.
2. The passage is a prophecy, concerning the future of
   Damascus.
3. Damascus will be utterly destroyed.
4. Damascus will no longer be a livable, inhabitable city.
5. Damascus will lie in ruins."[3]

Most would agree in general with Rosenberg's summary of
the meaning of this prophecy. The main disputed issue in Isaiah
17 is the timing of its fulfillment. Was it fulfilled sometime in

the past, or is its fulfillment still future? I don't have space here to deal with every point related to this issue, but I want to briefly summarize the key arguments for each view.

VIEW #1: THE DESTRUCTION OF DAMASCUS IN ISAIAH 17 IS FUTURE

The main contention of those who believe the fulfillment of Isaiah 17 is still future is simply that Damascus has never been removed from being a city. The city of Damascus is the capital of Syria today with a population of about 2.5 million. Since this prophecy must be literally fulfilled, they maintain it must refer to future destruction. Joel Rosenberg holds that Isaiah 17 refers to a future, possibly imminent, annihilation of Damascus.

Here's why Rosenberg believes this prophecy is future:

> When viewed together, we can say the following about the prophecies concerning Damascus found in Isaiah 17 and Jeremiah 49:
>
> a. The prophecies refer to a divine judgment by God against the city of Damascus. . . .
>
> b. The prophecies refer to the utter, catastrophic destruction of Damascus.
>
> c. Both are eschatological passages, referring to End Times events that have yet to occur.
>
> i. Isaiah's prophecy was given to him in 715 BC, well after the conquering of Damascus in 732 by Tiglath-pileser.

ii. Likewise, Jeremiah's ministry occurred between 626 BC and 586 BC, long after Tiglath-pileser conquered Damascus in 732 BC.

d. Damascus has certainly been attacked, conquered, and burned at various points in history, including Biblical history—but it is clear that the prophecies of Isaiah 17 and Jeremiah 49 have not yet been fulfilled. Damascus is, after all, one of the oldest continuously inhabited cities on the planet.

e. We cannot be certain when these judgments will happen, and the prophecies will be fulfilled.

f. They could come to pass before, during or after the War of Gog & Magog (Ezekiel 38–39); before, during, or after the Rapture; or before or during the Tribulation. The texts simply do not say, so we cannot be definitive.

g. It is possibly that the prophecies could come to pass in the not-too-distant future. But they certainly will come to pass at some point before the Second Coming of Christ (the "Day of the Lord.")[4]

Another writer describes his view of the final destruction of Damascus in the end times.

In the last days, the Bible tells us of a horrible series of events that will take place in the lands of Israel and Syria. One of these events is the disappearance of Damascus as one of the premiere cities in the world. . . .

In the very near future, Damascus will once again play a major role in human events. The prophet Isaiah provides us with God's commentary on a future conflict between Damascus and Israel, and in so doing, he reveals certain prophecies which have been partially fulfilled in the past. However, the ultimate fulfillment of Isaiah 17 remains in the future. The current existence of Damascus, which will one day cease to be a city, as well as the historical absence of the coalition of nations prophesied to attack Israel and be destroyed by God, is proof that Isaiah 17 prophesies events yet future.[5]

While Joel Rosenberg and others who hold a futurist view of these prophecies make some good points, and I appreciate their careful study and interaction with the text, I believe the prophecies of Damascus' destruction have already been fulfilled.

VIEW #2: THE DESTRUCTION OF DAMASCUS IN ISAIAH 17 IS PAST

Joel Rosenberg and those who agree with his position note that the entire message to the nations in Isaiah 13–24 is related to events in the end times. He concluded:

> In Isaiah 13 to Isaiah 24, the Lord speaks directly to the future of Gentile nations near or surrounding Israel. These prophecies are also End Times matters—that is, they are events that will take place just before the Tribulation, or during the Tribulation, and come to complete fulfillment on or about the

Day of the Lord (the literal, physical Second Coming of the Lord Jesus Christ).

We know these are End Times prophecies—and not near-term prophecies that would take place during Isaiah's lifetime or even in the generations that would immediately follow—because of the numerous eschatological references that Isaiah makes.[6]

I agree that many parts of Isaiah 13–24 are eschatological, but not everything. Isaiah 16:14 refers to the destruction of Moab "within three years." Isaiah 21:16 says, "In a year, as a hired man would count it, all the splendor of Kedar will terminate." These prophecies clearly have a very near fulfillment in view.

While much can be said on this issue, my main reason for viewing Isaiah 17 as fulfilled in the past is the *immediate* context. In the verses just before Isaiah 17:1, Isaiah prophesies the destruction of ancient Moab and says it will occur "within three years" (Isaiah 16:14). This clearly sets the fulfillment of this oracle in the very near future.

Then, in the final verses of Isaiah 17, the prophet looks ahead to the total destruction of the Assyrian army in one night (Isaiah 17:12–14). This was fulfilled in 701 BC when the army of Sennacherib, numbering 185,000, was killed by one angel on a single night as they camped in the land of Judah (Isaiah 37:36).

The immediate context of Isaiah 17:1–2 is telling and exerts a controlling influence on our interpretation. The prophecy of the destruction of Damascus is bracketed by two prophecies of events that were fulfilled within a few years of the time they were given.

Since the context *before* Isaiah 17:1–2 is a near future fulfillment and the context *after* it is also a near fulfillment, it would be strange for Isaiah 17:1–2 to have a distant fulfillment in the end times.

Isaiah 16:14 Prophecy of Moab's Destruction (fulfilled within three years)

Isaiah 17:1–11 Prophecy of the Destruction of Damascus

Isaiah 17:12–14 Prophecy of the Destruction of the Assyrian army in one night (fulfilled within about thirty years in 701 BC)

If the prophecy of the destruction of Damascus has already been literally fulfilled, when did it occur? I believe it was fulfilled in 732 BC when Damascus was destroyed by the Assyrians under the reign of Tiglath-pileser. The text never says that Damascus will be removed "forever" from being a city, only that it would be removed from being a city. Isaiah 17 prophesies a temporary desolation of Damascus like what happened to many nations and cities in the ancient Near East when they were razed by invading armies. Isaiah does not say that the city would never be rebuilt or inhabited again. It was leveled, uninhabited for a while, and then eventually rebuilt and inhabited again.

Warren Wiersbe supports this view of the timing: "In 17:1–2, he warned Damascus, the capital city of Aram (Syria), that the city would be taken by the enemy. This occurred when the Assyrians conquered Aram in 732 BC. Following their usual custom, the Assyrians deported many of the citizens, which left the land and cities deserted."[7]

JEREMIAH 49 AND DAMASCUS

The prophet Jeremiah penned his prophecy about God's judgment on Damascus about one hundred years after Isaiah. When Jeremiah prophesied, the Assyrian threat was gone. The main threat to the ancient Near East in Jeremiah's day was the Babylonian Empire under the rule of Nebuchadnezzar. Jeremiah's prophecy about the destruction of Damascus is found in Jeremiah 49:23–27.

Concerning Damascus.

"Hamath and Arpad are put to shame,

For they have heard bad news;

They are disheartened.

There is anxiety by the sea,

It cannot be calmed.

"Damascus has become helpless;

She has turned away to flee,

And panic has gripped her;

Distress and pangs have taken hold of her

Like a woman in childbirth.

How the city of praise has not been deserted,

the town of My joy!

Therefore, her young men will fall in her streets,

and all the men of war will be silenced in that day," declares

the Lord of hosts.

"I will set fire to the wall of Damascus,

And it will devour the fortified towers of Ben-hadad."

I believe this prophecy was fulfilled during the reign of King Nebuchadnezzar of Babylon when he conquered Aram or Syria.[8] These verses vividly describe the fear and panic that gripped the people of Damascus as the Babylonian army advanced.

John Walvoord agreed that the Damascus prophecies in Isaiah 17 and Jeremiah have been fulfilled.

> Damascus was one of the most ancient cities of the Middle East and one of the few to have a continuous history down to modern times. First mentioned in Genesis 14:15, it continued to have a relationship to Israel throughout the Old Testament period where there are more than forty references and in the New Testament where it is mentioned fifteen times. The more extended prophecies as found in Isaiah 17:1–14 and Jeremiah 49:23–27 have all been fulfilled as well as the occasional references found in Isaiah 7:8; 8:4; Amos 1:3–5; 3:12; 5:27.[9]

SYRIA'S FUTURE

While I believe the prophecies of Isaiah 17 and Jeremiah 49 concerning Damascus were fulfilled centuries ago, nevertheless I believe what's happening today in Syria is prophetically significant. Syria's rise to prominence is no accident. It's happening right on schedule in concert with many other important geopolitical developments. Syria serves as a major staging ground for some of the key events that are paving the way for outbreak of the end times.

Iran and Russia are amassing troops and military assets in Syria. Turkey is seeking control of northern Syria. All this converging activity right on Israel's border by nations listed in Ezekiel 38 is astounding. Israel's end-time enemies are literally gathered on Israel's northern doorstep. It's difficult to see how these conditions could persist much longer without creating some major shock waves.

Additionally, Syria is probably part of the inclusive, catch-all phrase "many peoples with you" in Ezekiel 38:6 that indicates others will join the Russian-Iranian invasion of Israel. This gives added importance to what we see in Syria. I believe what's currently happening in Syria carries great prophetic weight on several levels in light of Ezekiel 38 and the upsurge of Iran. The main members of the Gog coalition are all present on Syrian soil. Few developments are more prophetically significant than that.

We should keep our eyes on Syria as the buildup to the end accelerates.

APPENDIX 3

EZEKIEL 38 AND 39

EZEKIEL 38

And the word of the LORD came to me saying, "Son of man, set your face toward Gog of the land of Magog, the prince of Rosh, Meshech and Tubal, and prophesy against him and say, 'Thus says the Lord GOD, "Behold, I am against you, O Gog, prince of Rosh, Meshech and Tubal. I will turn you about and put hooks into your jaws, and I will bring you out, and all your army, horses and horsemen, all of them splendidly attired, a great company with buckler and shield, all of them wielding swords; Persia, Ethiopia and Put with them, all of them with shield and helmet; Gomer with all its troops; Beth-togarmah from the remote parts of the north with all its troops—many peoples with you.

"Be prepared, and prepare yourself, you and all your companies that are assembled about you, and be a guard for them. After many days you will be summoned; in the latter years you will come into the land that is restored from the sword, whose inhabitants have been gathered from many nations to the mountains of Israel which had been a continual waste; but its people were brought out from the nations, and they are living securely, all of them. You will go up, you will come like a storm; you will be like a cloud covering the land, you and all your troops, and many peoples with you."

'Thus says the Lord GOD, "It will come about on that day, that thoughts will come into your mind and you will devise an evil plan, and you will say, 'I will go up against the land of unwalled villages. I will go against those who are at rest, that live securely, all of them living without walls and having no bars or gates, to capture spoil and to seize plunder, to turn your hand against the waste places which are now inhabited, and against the people who are gathered from the nations, who have acquired cattle and goods, who live at the center of the world.' Sheba and Dedan and the merchants of Tarshish with all its villages will say to you, 'Have you come to capture spoil? Have you assembled your company to seize plunder, to carry away silver and gold, to take away cattle and goods, to capture great spoil?'"'

"Therefore prophesy, son of man, and say to Gog, 'Thus says the Lord GOD, "On that day when My people Israel are living securely, will you not know it? You will come from your place out of the remote parts of the north, you and many peoples with you, all of them riding on horses, a great assembly and a mighty army; and you will come up against My people Israel like a cloud to cover the land. It shall come about in the last days that I will bring you against My land, so that the nations may know Me when I am sanctified through you before their eyes, O Gog."

'Thus says the Lord GOD, "Are you the one of whom I spoke in former days through My servants the prophets of Israel, who prophesied in those days for many years that I would bring you against them? It will come about on that day, when Gog comes against the land of Israel," declares the Lord GOD, "that My fury will mount up in My anger. In My zeal and in My blazing wrath I declare that on that day there will surely be a great earthquake in the land of Israel. The fish of the sea, the birds of the heavens, the beasts of the field, all the creeping things that creep on the earth, and all the men who are on the face of the earth will shake at My presence; the mountains also will be thrown down, the steep pathways will collapse and every wall will fall to the ground. I will call for a sword against him on all My mountains," declares the Lord GOD. "Every man's sword will be against his brother. With pestilence and with blood I will enter into judgment with him; and I will rain on him and on his troops, and on the many peoples who are with him, a torrential rain, with hailstones, fire and brimstone. I will magnify Myself, sanctify Myself, and make Myself known in the sight of many nations; and they will know that I am the LORD."'

EZEKIEL 39

"And you, son of man, prophesy against Gog and say, 'Thus says the Lord GOD, "Behold, I am against you, O Gog, prince of Rosh, Meshech and Tubal; and I will turn you around, drive you on, take you up from the remotest parts of the north and bring you against the mountains of Israel. I will strike your bow from your left hand and dash down your arrows from your right hand. You will fall on the mountains of Israel, you and all your troops and the peoples who are with you; I will give you as food to every kind of predatory bird and beast of the field. You will fall on the open field; for it is I who have spoken," declares the Lord God. "And I will send fire upon Magog and those who inhabit the coastlands in safety; and they will know that I am the Lord.

"My holy name I will make known in the midst of My people Israel; and I will not let My holy name be profaned anymore. And the nations will know that I am the Lord, the Holy One in Israel. Behold, it is coming and it shall be done," declares the Lord God. "That is the day of which I have spoken.

"Then those who inhabit the cities of Israel will go out and make fires with the weapons and burn them, both shields and bucklers, bows and arrows, war clubs and spears, and for seven years they will make fires of them. They will not take wood from the field or gather firewood from the forests, for they will make fires with the weapons; and they will take the spoil of those who despoiled them and seize the plunder of those who plundered them," declares the Lord God.

"On that day I will give Gog a burial ground there in Israel, the valley of those who pass by east of the sea, and it will block off those who would pass by. So they will bury Gog there with all his horde, and they will call it the valley of Hamon-gog. For seven months the house of Israel will be burying them in order to cleanse the land. Even all the people of the land will bury them; and it will be to their renown on the day that I glorify Myself," declares the Lord GOD. "They will set apart men who will constantly pass through the land, burying those who were passing through, even those left on the surface of the ground, in order to cleanse it. At the end of seven months they will make a search. As those who pass through the land pass through and anyone sees a man's bone, then he will set up a marker by it until the buriers have buried it in the valley of Hamon-gog. And even the name of the city will be Hamonah. So they will cleanse the land."'

"As for you, son of man, thus says the Lord GOD, 'Speak to every kind of bird and to every beast of the field, "Assemble and come, gather from every side to My sacrifice which I am going to sacrifice for you, as a great sacrifice on the mountains of Israel, that you may eat flesh and drink blood. You will eat the flesh of mighty men and drink the blood of the princes of the earth, as though they were rams, lambs, goats and bulls, all of them fatlings of Bashan. So you will eat fat until you are glutted, and drink blood until you are drunk, from My sacrifice which I have sacrificed for you. You will be glutted at My table with horses and charioteers, with mighty men and all the men of war," declares the Lord GOD.

"And I will set My glory among the nations; and all the nations will see My judgment which I have executed and My hand which I have laid on them. And the house of Israel will know that I am the LORD their God from that day onward. The nations will know that the house of Israel went into exile for their iniquity because they acted treacherously against Me, and I hid My face from them; so I gave them into the hand of their adversaries, and all of them fell by the sword. According to their uncleanness and according to their transgressions I dealt with them, and I hid My face from them.""""

Therefore thus says the Lord God, "Now I will restore the fortunes of Jacob and have mercy on the whole house of Israel; and I will be jealous for My holy name. They will forget their disgrace and all their treachery which they perpetrated against Me, when they live securely on their own land with no one to make them afraid. When I bring them back from the peoples and gather them from the lands of their enemies, then I shall be sanctified through them in the sight of the many nations. Then they will know that I am the Lord their God because I made them go into exile among the nations, and then gathered them again to their own land; and I will leave none of them there any longer. I will not hide My face from them any longer, for I will have poured out My Spirit on the house of Israel," declares the Lord God.

NOTES

Beyond the Headlights

1. Charles Dyer and Mark Tobey, *Clash of Kingdoms: What the Bible Says About Russia, ISIS, Iran, and the End Times* (Nashville, TN: Thomas Nelson, 2017), 42–44.

Chapter 1: Countdown to Crisis

1. Sebastien Roblin, "Fact: The United States and Iran Came Within Minutes of War Back in June," *The National Interest*, November 2, 2019, https://nationalinterest.org/blog/buzz /fact-united-states-and-iran-came-within-minutes-war-back -june-93011.

2. Steven Simon and Jonathan Stevenson, "Iran: The Case Against War," *New York Review of Books*, August 15, 2019, https://www .nybooks.com/articles/2019/08/15/iran-case-against-war/.

3. Lara Seligman, "Top US General: It's 'Very Possible' Iran Will Attack Again," *Foreign Policy*, November 23, 2019, https:// foreignpolicy.com/2019/11/23/very-possible-iran-will-attack -again-top-us-general-says/.

4. https://abcnews.go.com/WNT/video/shootdown-showdown-us -iran-63848747.

5. Robin Wright, "Trump Launches 'Game of Thrones' Showdown with Iran," *New Yorker*, November 5, 2018, https://www.newyorker.com/news/news-desk/trump-launches-game-of-thrones-showdown-with-iran.

6. David Brennan, "Any Country Hosting US Troops May Be Targeted by Iran in the Event of War, Military Says," *Newsweek*, November 4, 2019, https://www.newsweek.com/country-hosting-u-s-troops-targeted-iran-war-military-allies-middle-east-proxies-abolfazl-shekarchi-1469588.

7. "Trump Finally Fires Back at Iran," *Wall Street Journal*, December 29, 2019, https://www.wsj.com/articles/trump-finally-fires-back-at-iran-11577662029.

8. Jim Hanson, "Jim Hanson: US Should Attack Iran in Response to Attack on Our Embassy in Iraq," Fox News, December 31, 2019, https://www.foxnews.com/opinion/jim-hanson-us-must-take-military-action-against-iran-in-response-to-attack-on-our-embassy-in-iraq.

9. Lucas Tomlinson, "Up to 4,000 US Troops Could Deploy to Middle East Amid Baghdad Unrest: Officials," Fox News, December 31, 2019, https://www.foxnews.com/politics/troops-middle-east-baghdad-embassy-kuwait.

10. Fred Kaplan, "Trump Just Declared War on Iran," Slate.com, January 3, 2020, https://slate.com/news-and-politics/2020/01/soleimani-trump-muhandis-iran-iraq.html.

11. Chris Kahn, "Americans Increasingly Critical of Trump's Record on Iran, Most Expect War: Reuters/Ipsos Poll," *Reuters*, January 7, 2020, https://www.reuters.com/article/us-usa-trump-iran-poll/americans-increasingly-critical-of-trumps-record-on-iran-most-expect-war-reuters-ipsos-poll-idUSKBN1Z62KF.

12. Thomas L. Friedman, "Trump and Tehran Shake Up the Middle East," *New York Times*, October 8, 2019, https://www.nytimes.com/2019/10/08/opinion/iran-israel-saudi-arabia.html.

13. Paul LeBlanc, Kylie Atwood, Jeremy Diamond, and Sarah Westwood, "Trump: US 'Locked and Loaded Depending on Verification' of Attack on Saudi Oil Field," CNN Politics, September 16, 2019, https://www.cnn.com/2019/09/15/politics /trump-us-saudi-arabia-attack-iran-iraq/index.html.

14. Sune Engel Rasmussen, Ghassan Adnan, and Nazih Osseiran, "Iran Finds Itself in Crosshairs of Arab Protesters," *Wall Street Journal*, November 4, 2019, https://www.wsj.com/articles/iran -finds-itself-in-cross-hairs-of-arab-protesters-11572890538.

15. David Rosenthal, *Zion's Fire*, March–April 2019.

16. Yonah Jeremy Bob, "Ex-Security Chief: Israel Needs to Attack Iran to Stop Nukes, 'Ring of Fire,'" *Jerusalem Post*, November 11, 2019, https://www.jpost.com/Israel-News/Israel-will-need-to -attack-Iran-to-block-nuke-umbrella-ring-of-fire-607533.

17. Judah Ari Gross, "Top Israeli Think Tank Warns: Potential for War with Iran Is Growing," *Times of Israel*, January 6, 2020, https://www.timesofisrael.com/top-israeli-think-tank-warns -potential-for-war-with-iran-is-growing/.

18. Seth Cropsey, "For the US and Israel, a Strike Against Iran Seems Inevitable," *The Hill*, October 22, 2019, https://thehill .com/opinion/national-security/466842-for-the-us-and-israel-a -strike-against-iran-seems-inevitable.

19. Thomas L. Friedman, "Trump and Tehran Shake Up the Middle East," *New York Times*, October 8, 2019, https://www .nytimes.com/2019/10/08/opinion/iran-israel-saudi-arabia.html.

20. Yossef Bodansky, "Iran Prepares for War with Israel," *Oil Price*, October 21, 2019, https://oilprice.com/Energy/Energy-General /Iran-Prepares-For-War-With-Israel.html.

Chapter 2: Atomic Iran and the Apocalypse

1. *Meet the Press*, transcript for April 2, 2006, NBC News, http:// www.nbcnews.com/id/12067487/print/1/displaymode/1098/.

2. Ehud Yaari, "How Iran Plans to Destroy Israel," *American Interest*, August 1, 2015, https://www.the-american-interest .com/2015/08/01/how-iran-plans-to-destroy-israel/.

3. Eric Brewer and Ariane Tabatabai, "Understanding Iran's Nuclear Escalation Strategy," *War on the Rocks*, December 12, 2019, https://warontherocks.com/2019/12/understanding-irans -nuclear-escalation-strategy/.

4. "Iran President Says Country Testing New Faster Centrifuges," *New York Times*, December 19, 2019.

5. Tovah Lazaroff, "Mike Pompeo: Iran Positioning Itself for Rapid Nuclear Break-out," *Jerusalem Post*, November 7, 2019, https://www.jpost.com/Middle-East/Pompeo-All-nations-must -pressure-Iran-due-to-their-nuclear-extortion-607166.

6. Yonah Jeremy Bob, "Ex-Security Chief: Israel Needs to Attack Iran to Stop Nukes, 'Ring of Fire,'" *Jerusalem Post*, November 11, 2019, https://www.jpost.com/Israel-News/Israel-will-need-to -attack-Iran-to-block-nuke-umbrella-ring-of-fire-607533.

7. For an exhaustive overview of Iran's nuclear history, see "Iran's Nuclear Capabilities Fast Facts," CNN, May 26, 2019, https:// www.cnn.com/2013/11/07/world/meast/irans-nuclear -capabilities-fast-facts/index.html.

8. Jeffery Goldberg, "The Iranian Regime on Israel's Right to Exist," *Atlantic*, March 9, 2015, https://www.theatlantic.com /international/archive/2015/03/Iranian-View-of-Israel/387085/.

9. "Israel Should Be Annihilated, Iranian Official Says," *Jerusalem Post*, August 25, 2015, https://www.jpost.com/Middle-East /Iran/Israel-should-be-annihilated-Iranian-official-says-413212.

10. Claire Anderson, "US-Iran Crisis: Pompeo Sends Chilling Warning to Iran—'Time Is Running Out,'" *Daily Express*, August 13, 2019, https://www.express.co.uk/news/world /1164992/US-iran-news-world-war-3-latest-mike-pompeo -Qasem-Soleimani-travel-ban-terror-irgc.

11. "Trump Finally Fires Back at Iran," *Wall Street Journal*, December 29, 2019, https://www.wsj.com/articles/trump -finally-fires-back-at-iran-11577662029.

12. Michael Oren, "The Coming Middle East Conflagration," *Atlantic*, November 4, 2019, https://www.theatlantic.com /ideas/archive/2019/11/israel-preparing-open-war/601285/.

13. Joseph Krauss, "'Days of God': A look at Iran's mounting crises, Associated Press, January 17, 2020, https://apnews.com /b8a52757804b5787013a568b2cbc3521.

14. "Iran and America in 2020: A Dreadful Relationship," *Economist*, December 25, 2019, https://www.economist .com/the-world-in/2019/12/25/iran-and-america-in-2020 -a-dreadful-relationship.

15. Lela Gilbert, "Iran's Aggression and the Shi'ite Apocalypse," *Jerusalem Post*, August 17, 2019, https://www.jpost.com /Opinion/Irans-aggression-and-the-Shiite-apocalypse-598904.

16. "Jack Cohen–The Sh'ite Apocalyptic Vision," August 21, 2019, https://israelseen.com/2019/08/21/jack-cohen-the-shite -apocalyptic-vision/. The following is an excellent summary of the difference between Shia and Sunni Islam: Shi'ism results from the beginning of Islam, when after Mohammed died in 632 he had not named a successor. As a result, his immediate followers decided to elect chief among them Abu Bakr as Caliph, both as spiritual and temporal leader. These became the Sunni Muslims. However, there were many who thought his successor should be a blood relative, and his only surviving blood relative was his grandson Ali, son of his daughter Fatimah and son-in-law Hussein. His followers became the Shia. After Mohammed's death the Sunni Muslims raised an army and began their series of conquests, including Damascus in 634, Jerusalem in 639, and North Africa in 652. The inevitable Sunni-Shia clash came at Karbala in what is now Iraq in 680 when the Shia army under

Ali were defeated by a much larger Sunni army under the Caliph. From then on the Shia were a persecuted heretical minority of Islam that developed its own culture. Although there are several sub-sects of Shia Islam, the majority and that practiced in Iran is what is known as "Twelver" Islam. They believe that after the death of Ali there were ten other Imams, who were his descendants and for the most part were secret. But, the Twelfth Imam is the Mahdi or savior (obviously derived from the Judaic concept of the Messiah that Christianity also adopted) known as the Hidden Imam. The Twelver Shia, i.e., the Iranians and their proxies, believe that at the end of days when the hidden Imam appears there will be an apocalyptic bloody conflict between the Muslim believers (i.e., the Shia) and the infidels, which of course the Shia will win.

17. Salman Masalha, "Iran's Messianic War," *Haaretz*, January 6, 2018, https://www.haaretz.com/opinion/.premium-irans -messianic-war-1.5729488.

Chapter 3: Dire Straits

1. https://www.thefreedictionary.com/dire+straits.

2. Melissa Etehad, "What's Behind Iran's Actions in the Strait of Hormuz?" *Los Angeles Times*, July 19, 2019, https://www.latimes .com/world-nation/story/2019-07-19/iran-strait-of-hormuz-oil -tanker-seizure.

3. Ilan Goldenberg, Jessica, Schwed, and Kaleigh Thomas, "In Dire Straits? Implications of US-Iran Tensions for the Global Oil Market," Center on Global Energy Policy, November 21, 2019, https://energypolicy.columbia.edu/research/report/dire -straits-implications-us-iran-tensions-global-oil-market.

4. "Iran Tanker Seizure: What Is the Strait of Hormuz?" *BBC News*, July 29, 2019, https://www.bbc.com/news/world-middle-east -49070882.

5. Ramtin Arablouei and Rund Abdelfatah, "Remembering the 'Tanker War' of the 1980s," NPR, August 1, 2019, https://www .npr.org/2019/08/01/747170673/remembering-the-tanker-war -of-the-1980s.

6. Alex Winston, "Iran Navy Chief: Zionist Presence in Persian Gulf May Trigger War," *Jerusalem Post*, August 12, 2019, https:// www.jpost.com/Israel-News/Iran-Navy-Chief -Zionist-presence-in-Persian-Gulf-may-trigger-war-598415.

7. Robin Wright, "Iran's Eye-for-an-Eye Strategy in the Gulf," *New Yorker*, July 19, 2019, https://www.newyorker.com/news /our-columnists/irans-eye-for-an-eye-strategy-in-the-gulf.

Chapter 5: The Aligning of Nations

1. http://www.quotationspage.com/quote/31806.html.

2. Dyer and Tobey, *Clash of Kingdoms*, 46.

3. Joel C. Rosenberg, "Putin Rising: But Is He "Gog"? Joel C. Rosenberg's Blog, August 17, 2011, https://flashtrafficblog .allisrael.com/2011/08/17/putin-rising-but-is-he-gog/.

4. Thomas Grove, "Czar Vladimir? Putin Acolytes Want to Bring Back the Monarchy," *Wall Street Journal*, December 13, 2018, https://www.wsj.com/articles/czar-vladimir-putin-acolytes -want-to-bring-back-the-monarchy-11544732680.

5. Lawk Ghafuri, "Putin Is 'King' of Middle East: Former French Minister," *Rudaw*, November 19, 2019, https://www.rudaw.net /english/kurdistan/191120191.

6. Jonathan Spyer, "Putin Is the New King of Syria," *Wall Street Journal*, October 16, 2019, https://www.wsj.com/articles/putin -is-the-new-king-of-syria-11571264222.

7. Josephus, *Antiquities* 1.6.1.

8. The Hebrew scholar Gesenius identified Rosh as Russia. Gesenius, *Gesenius' Hebrew-Chaldee Lexicon to the Old Testament* (Grand Rapids, MI: Eerdmans, 1949), 752. For an

excellent presentation of the grammatical and philological support for taking Rosh as a place name, see James D. Price, "Rosh: An Ancient Land Known to Ezekiel," *Grace Theological Journal* 6 (1985): 67–89; Clyde E. Billington, Jr., "The Rosh People in History and Prophecy (Part One)," *Michigan Theological Journal* 3 (1992): 55–64; Clyde E. Billington Jr., "The Rosh People in History and Prophecy (Part Two)" *Michigan Theological Journal* 3 (1992): 143–174; Clyde E. Billington Jr., "The Rosh People in History and Prophecy (Part Three)," *Michigan Theological Journal* 4 (1993): 39–62; Jon Mark Ruthven and Ihab Griess, *The Prophecy That Is Shaping History: New Research on Ezekiel's Vision of the End* (Longwood, FL: Xulon Press, 2003), 61–62.

9. Katie Sanders, " Did Vladimir Putin Call the Breakup of the USSR 'The Greatest Geopolitical Tragedy of the 20th Century?'" politifact.com, March 6, 2014, https://www.politifact .com/punditfact/statements/2014/mar/06/john-bolton/did -vladimir-putin-call-breakup-ussr-greatest-geop/.

10. "Turkey Speeds Up Libya Troop Deployment Deal to Prevent Slide into 'Chaos,'" *Reuters*, December 29, 2019, https://www .reuters.com/article/us-turkey-libya-minister/turkey-speeds-up -libya-troop-deployment-deal-to-prevent-slide-into-chaos -idUSKBN1YX040.

11. Josephus, *Antiquities* 1.6.1. Yamauchi provides a thorough description of the ancient Scythians. Edwin M. Yamauchi, *Foes from the Northern Frontier* (Grand Rapids, MI: Baker, 1992), 64–109.

12. "Turkey Opposed to Anyone That Stands by Israel, says Erdoğan," *Ahval News*, July 29, 2019, https://ahvalnews.com /turkey-israel/turkey-opposed-anyone-stands-israel-says-erdogan.

13. "Turkey Opposed to Anyone That Stands by Israel, says Erdoğan," *Ahval News*, July 29, 2019.

14. Seth J. Frantzman, "State Media in Iran, Russia Indicate Growing Russia-Iran-Turkey Alliance," *Jerusalem Post*, September 26, 2019, https://www.jpost.com/Middle-East/State-media-in-Iran-Russia -indicate-growing-Russia-Iran-Turkey-alliance-602787.

15. Frantzman, "State Media in Iran, Russia Indicate Growing Russia-Iran-Turkey Alliance," *Jerusalem Post*, September 26, 2019.

16. Arnold Fruchtenbaum, *The Footsteps of the Messiah: A Study of the Sequence of Prophetic Events*, rev. ed. (Tustin, CA: Ariel Ministries, 2003), 111–112. A place known as Tarshish was located on the east coast of Africa, although the exact location is not known. Some place Tarshish in England and from this view they argue that the merchants of Tarshish are the colonies and eventually the nations that rose from England. This view is used to identify the United States as the "young lions of Tarshish." I reject this view. It's far too tenuous to use this cryptic phrase to find America in Ezekiel's prophecy.

17. John Phillips, *Exploring the Future: A Comprehensive Guide to Bible Prophecy* (Grand Rapids, MI: Kregel, 2003), 316.

18. Joel C. Rosenberg, "Putin Rising: But Is He 'Gog'?" Joel C. Rosenberg's Blog, August 17, 2011, https://flashtrafficblog .allisrael.com/2011/08/17/putin-rising-but-is-he-gog/.

Chapter 6: Final Showdown: The War of Gog and Magog

1. "D-Day Fast Facts," June 11, 2019, https://www.cnn.com/2013 /06/03/world/europe/d-day-fast-facts/index.html.

2. Walter C. Kaiser, Jr., *Preaching and Teaching the Last Things: Old Testament Eschatology for the Life of the Church* (Grand Rapids, MI: Baker Academic, 2011), 90.

3. Kaiser, *Preaching and Teaching the Last Things*, 89–90.

4. Joel C. Rosenberg, *Epicenter: Why the Current Rumblings in the Middle East Will Change Your Future* (Carol Stream, IL: Tyndale, 2006), 165.

5. Putting this invasion before the rapture is problematic because Ezekiel places the invasion in the "latter years" (Ezekiel 38:8) and "last days" (Ezekiel 38:16) of Israel's history. While the church is still on the earth, God's final program for Israel will still be on hold. The latter years for Israel will begin with the Tribulation period.

6. One reason these two events are equated by some is because they both mention a great bird supper (Ezekiel 39:17–21 and Revelation 19:17–18). The main problem with equating Ezekiel 38 with the Battle of Armageddon is that Ezekiel says the invasion will occur at a time when Israel is "at rest" and "living securely." Armageddon occurs at the end of the Tribulation, which is one time when Israel will be in danger. Placing Ezekiel 38 at the end of the Tribulation fails to meet this chronological marker in Ezekiel 38.

7. The only mention of Gog and Magog outside Ezekiel 38–39 is Revelation 20:8. For this reason, equating these two passages is viewed by many as the simplest solution to the timing of the invasion in Ezekiel 38. However, two points argue against equating these two passages. First, Ezekiel 38 lists specific nations that will come against Israel, while Revelation 20 refers to all nations. Second, Ezekiel 38–39 occurs before the coming millennium and time of Israel's final restoration while Revelation 20:8 comes after the one-thousand-year reign of Christ on earth described in Revelation 20:1–6. This raises an interesting question. If these are two different battles, separated from each other by more than one thousand years, then why are they both called Gog and Magog? The preferred explanation is that John uses the phrase from the Old Testament in a summary fashion, like we might use the word *Waterloo*. Or John may employ this term in the same way we tie together two great wars involving the same location as World War I and World War II. John's use of "Gog and Magog"

signals to anyone familiar with the Old Testament that he's describing an all-out war against God and His people where the invaders are obliterated by supernatural intervention.

8. John F. Walvoord, *The Nations in Prophecy* (Grand Rapids, MI: Zondervan, 1967), 110.

9. David Jeremiah, *Is This the End?* (Nashville, TN: Thomas Nelson, 2016), 226.

10. Walvoord, *The Nations in Prophecy*, 110.

11. Walvoord, *The Nations in Prophecy*, 115.

12. Warren W. Wiersbe, *The Wiersbe Bible Commentary: Old Testament* (Colorado Springs, CO: David C. Cook, 2007), 1334.

13. https://www.goodreads.com/quotes/14977-i-know-not-with -what-weapons-world-war-iii-will.

14. Charles C. Ryrie, *The Ryrie Study Bible* (Chicago, IL: Moody, 1995), footnote on page 1,326.

15. Christopher J. H. Wright, *The Message of Ezekiel, The Bible Speaks Today*, ed. J. A. Motyer (Downers Grove, IL: IVP Academic, 2001), 322.

Chapter 7: Israel and Iran at War

1. Adrian Rogers, *Unveiling the End Times in Our Time* (Nashville, TN: B & H, 2004), 142.

2. Charles H. Dyer, *World News and Bible Prophecy* (Wheaton, IL: Tyndale, n.d.), 13.

3. "Top Iran General Says Destroying Israel 'Achievable Goal,'" *Daily Mail*, September 30, 2019, https://www.dailymail.co.uk /news/article-7520939/Top-Iranian-general-says-destroying -Israel-achievable-goal.html.

4. Anna Ahronheim, "Senior Iranian Commander: the Islamic Republic Is on Israel's Border," *Jerusalem Post*, August 5, 2019, https://www.jpost.com/Middle-East/Senior-Iranian -commander-The-Islamic-republic-is-on-Israels-borders-597725.

5. Quoted by David Rosenthal, "The Rise of Iran and the Emerging Shia Crescent," *Zion's Fire*, July–August 2019, 5.

6. Seth J. Frantzman, " Iran's Afghan Mercenaries Threaten Israel: Final Target Is the Golan," *Jerusalem Post*, December 24, 2019, https://www.jpost.com/Middle -EastIrans-Afghan-mercenaries-threaten-Israel-from -Golan-611967.

7. Amos Harel, "How Israel's Conflict with Iran Will Be Different in 2020," *Haaretz*, December 19, 2019, https://www.haaretz.com /israel-news/.premium-how-israel-s-conflict-with-iran-will-be -different-in-2020-1.8288492.

8. Gareth Narunsky, "Very Close to War with Iran," *Australian Jewish News*, November 15, 2019, https://ajn.timesofisrael.com /very-close-to-war-with-iran/.

9. Israel Hayom, "Iran: Israel Will Be Destroyed in 30 Minutes If We Are Attacked," July 1, 2019, https://www.israelhayom.com /2019/07/01/iran-israel-will-be-destroyed-in-30-minutes-if-we -are-attacked/.

10. Michael Oren, "The Coming Middle East Conflagration," *Atlantic*, November 4, 2019, https://www.theatlantic.com/ideas /archive/2019/11/israel-preparing-open-war/601285/.

11. Yaakov Katz, "How the Israel-Iran War Might Begin," *Jerusalem Post*, December 6, 2019, https://www.jpost.com /Opinion/Editors-Notes-How-the-Israel-Iran-war-might -begin-610029.

12. Katz, "How the Israel-Iran War Might Begin."

Chapter 8: Will America Survive?

1. Alexander Tyler and James Olson, "Democracy—and the Fall of the Athenian Republic," http://www.theroadtoemmaus. org/RdLb/21PbAr/Hst/US/DmocAthnsUS.htm (accessed November 19, 2019).

2. For a more in-depth discussion of the various views, see Mark Hitchcock, *The Late Great United States* (Colorado Springs, CO: Multnomah Books, 2009).

3. Joel Rosenberg, *Implosion: Can America Recover from Its Economic and Spiritual Challenges in Time?* (Carol Stream, IL: Tyndale, 2012), 125.

4. Mitchell Nemeth, "18 Facts on the US National Debt That Are Almost Too Hard to Believe," Foundation for Economic Education, September 17, 2019, https://fee.org/articles/18-facts-on-the-us-national-debt-that-are-almost-too-hard-to-believe/.

5. Jeff Kinley, *The End of America? Bible Prophecy and a Country in Crisis* (Eugene, OR: Harvest House, 2017), 104.

6. Kinley, *The End of America?*, 98.

7. Kinley, *The End of America?*, 104.

8. Julia Manchester, "Analyst Says US Is Most Divided Since Civil War," *The Hill*, October 3, 2018, https://thehill.com/hilltv/what-americas-thinking/409718-analyst-says-the-us-is-the-most-divided-since-the-civl-war.

9. Steve Chapman, "Is America More Politically Polarized than Ever? Not Quite," *Chicago Tribune*, September 21, 2018, https://www.chicagotribune.com/columns/steve-chapman/ct-perspec-chapman-polarized-america-civil-war-0923-20180921-story.html.

10. Aris Folley, "GOP Lawmaker Invokes Possibility of 'Civil War' After House Votes on Trump Impeachment Procedures," *The Hill*, October 31, 2019, https://thehill.com/homenews/house/468419-gop-lawmaker-invokes-civil-war-after-house-votes-on-trump-impeachment.

11. Bill O'Reilly, "The War over Donald Trump," Bill O'Reilly.com, September 26, 2019, https://www.billoreilly.com/b/The-War-Over-Donald-Trump/580335624758333012.html.

12. Jamie Seidel, "The Second US Civil War," news.com.au, January 6, 2019, https://www.news.com.au/lifestyle/real-life/news-life/the

-second-us-civil-war/news-story/ec43b36de5f5f9f11e478a8fc71
ea2dc.

13. "BU Historian Answers: Are We Headed for Another Civil
    War?" *BU Today*, March 27, 2019, http://www.bu.edu/articles
    /2019/are-we-headed-for-another-civil-war/.

14. Ryan W. Miller, "Poll: Almost a Third of US Voters Think a
    Second Civil War Is Coming Soon," *USA Today*, June 27, 2018,
    https://www.usatoday.com/story/news/politics/onpolitics/2018
    /06/27/civil-war-likely-voters-say-rasmussen-poll/740731002/.

15. Seidel, "The Second US Civil War."

16. Kinley, *The End of America?*, 193–97.

17. Kinley, *The End of America?*, 197–99.

Chapter 9: Hope for Today

1. Sebastian Kettley, "Nostradamus 2020 Predictions: WAR,
   Trump Impeachment and Rising Seas in the New Year," *Express*,
   January 4, 2019, https://www.express.co.uk/news/weird/1219799
   /Nostradamus-2020-predictions-world-war-3-Trump
   -impeachment-rising-seas-New-Year-prophecies.

2. Grace Hauck, "20 Predictions for 2020: Here's What People
   Said Would Happen by This Year," *USA Today*, December 22,
   2019, https://www.usatoday.com/story/news/nation/2019/12/22
   /2020-predictions-decades-ago-self-driving-cars-mars-voting
   /2594825001/.

3. Dr. David Jeremiah, *The Book of Signs: 31 Undeniable Prophecies
   of the Apocalypse* (Nashville, TN: Thomas Nelson, 2019), 42.

4. Jeremiah, *The Book of Signs*, 42–43.

5. Warren W. Wiersbe, *The Wiersbe Bible Commentary: Old Testament*
   (Colorado Springs, CO: David C. Cook, 2007), 1332–33.

6. Adapted from Robert J. Morgan, *Worry Less, Live More: God's
   Prescription for a Better Life* (Nashville, TN: Thomas Nelson,
   2017), 56–57.

7. Max Lucado, *Unshakable Hope* (Nashville, TN: Thomas Nelson, 2018), 10.

8. https://www.azquotes.com/quote/1184777.

9. Caleb Parke, "Iran Has the World's 'Fastest-Growing Church,' Despite No Buildings—And It's Mostly Led by Women," Fox News, September 27, 2019, https://www.foxnews.com/faith-values /worlds-fastest-growing-church-women-documentary-film.

10. Parke, "Iran Has the World's 'Fastest-Growing Church,' Despite No Buildings—And It's Mostly Led by Women," Fox News, September 27, 2019.

Appendix 1: The Elam Prophecies in Light of Current Events in Iran

1. Joel C. Rosenberg, "Notes on the Future of Damascus According to Bible Prophecy," updated: September 9, 2013, http://www.joelrosenberg.com/files/2013/09/STUDY -Damascus-prophecies-R.pdf.

2. Bill Salus, "Nuclear Iran: 'Are Ezekiel 38 (Persia) and Jeremiah 49 (Elam) the Same Prophecy?'" *Prophecy Depot*, April 30, 2018, http://www.prophecydepotministries.net/2018/nuclear-iran-are -ezekiel-38-persia-and-jeremiah-49-elam-the-same-prophecy/.

3. https://walvoord.com/book/export/html/318.

4. Charles L. Feinberg, "Jeremiah," *The Expositor's Bible Commentary*, gen. ed. Frank E. Gaebelein, vol. 6 (Grand Rapids, MI: Zondervan, 1986), 671.

5. Wiersbe, *The Wiersbe Bible Commentary: Old Testament*, 1259.

6. Salus, "Nuclear Iran: 'Are Ezekiel 38 (Persia) and Jeremiah 49 (Elam) the Same Prophecy?'" *Prophecy Depot*, April 30, 2018.

Appendix 2: Iran's Presence in Syria and the Destruction of Damascus in Isaiah 17

1. Trey Yingst, "Iran Building New Classified Military Base in Syria: Intelligence Sources," September 3, 2019, Fox News,

https://www.foxnews.com/world/iran-building-classified
-military-base-syria.

2. "Top Iranian Official: Israel 'Will Regret' Attacks in Syria," *Times of Israel*, December 23, 2019, https://www.timesofisrael .com/top-iranian-official-israel-will-regret-attacks-in-syria/.

3. Joel C. Rosenberg, "Notes on the Future of Damascus According to Bible Prophecy," updated: September 9, 2013, http://www.joelrosenberg.com/files/2013/09/STUDY -Damascus-prophecies-R.pdf.

4. Rosenberg, "Notes on the Future of Damascus According to Bible Prophecy." One point Rosenberg makes is that Isaiah 17 was prophesied in 715 BC, so it can't be a prophecy about the destruction of Damascus in 732 BC by the Assyrians. He gets this date from Isaiah 14:28, which refers to the "year that King Ahaz died" which was 715 BC. However, this is the date for the oracle against the Philistines in Isaiah 14:29–32, but there's no evidence it's the date for the oracle against Damascus three chapters later. So, there's nothing in the context to preclude the Assyrian destruction of Damascus in 732 BC from being the fulfillment of Isaiah's prophecy.

5. Britt Gillette, "Isaiah 17: Destruction of Damascus," Rapture Ready, November 15, 2011, https://www.raptureready.com /2011/11/15/isaiah-17-destruction-of-damascus-by-britt -gillette/.

6. Rosenberg, "Notes on the Future of Damascus According to Bible Prophecy."

7. Wiersbe, *The Wiersbe Bible Commentary: Old Testament*, 1166.

8. Charles H. Dyer, "Jeremiah," *The Bible Knowledge Commentary*, vol. 2, ed. John F. Walvoord and Roy B. Zuck (Wheaton, IL: Victor Books, 1985), 1198. Dyer notes the mention of "Ben-hadad," which "was the name of the dynasty that ruled in Damascus in the ninth and eighth centuries BC." The use of

that name would be strange if this refers to an end-time event. The towers of Ben-hadad are long gone today.

9. John F. Walvoord, "Chapter XV The Nations in the Millennium and the Eternal State," https://walvoord.com/article/306.

ABOUT THE AUTHOR

Mark Hitchcock has authored more than thirty books related to Bible prophecy. He has earned ThM and PhD degrees from Dallas Theological Seminary and is an associate professor there. He lives in Edmond, Oklahoma, with his wife, Cheryl, and serves as Senior Pastor of Faith Bible Church. He and his wife have two married sons and three grandchildren.